7/12

133.
333
UL

Please renew/return items by last date shown

So that your telephone call is charged at local rate, please call the numbers as set out below:

	From Area codes 01923 or 020:	From the rest of Hertfordshire:
Renewals:	01923 471373	01438 737373
Enquiries:	01923 471333	01438 737333
Textphone:	01923 471599	01438 737599

L32 www.hertsdirect.org/librarycatalogue

OTHER BOOKS BY THE AUTHOR

* The Chinese Dragon *
* Creating Prosperity *
* Tap the Power Inside You *
* Climb The Career Ladder with Confidence *

* Feng Shui *
* Applied Feng Shui *

First published June 1994
Secound printing July 1994
Third printing December 1994
Fourth printing August 1995
Fifth printing August 1995
Sixth printing January 1996
Seventh printing April 1996

Published by Konsep Lagenda Sdn Bhd.
Illustrations and Cover design by Lillian Too
Copyright 1994 Lillian Too
Printed by Ritz Print Sdn Bhd.

PRACTICAL APPLICATIONS OF
FENG SHUI

 LILLIAN TOO

BEST SELLING AUTHOR OF
FENG SHUI

and
APPLIED FENG SHUI

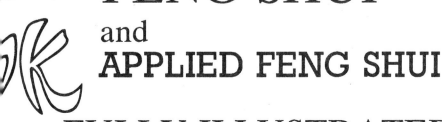

FULLY ILLUSTRATED

This is the third of Lillian Too's books on the practice and science of Feng Shui, an ancient Chinese wisdom that advocates living in harmony with nature and the environment, in the process tapping the Earth's energy to attract good luck, prosperity, abundant good health, wealth and happiness.

The first book served as a comprehensive introduction to FENG SHUI - familiarising the reader to its history, its origins and its background, and to the colourful symbolisms of this ancient science. Green dragon white tiger formations; black turtle hills and red phoenix footstools, the trapping of the cosmic chi, the danger of poison arrows, the potency of the Pa Kua symbol ... focusing the reader's attention on landscapes and the environmental influences on Feng Shui.

The second book revealed the secrets of the powerful PA KUA LO SHU FENG SHUI formula, a potent off shoot of the Compass School of Feng Shui, a formula which pinpoints each person's four auspicious and four inauspicious directions; and how these can be applied to one's homes and offices to align individual chi flows with that of one's surroundings and thereby tapping into the luck of the Earth and achieving abundant prosperity, and great wealth ... the highlight of the second book was to focus on a a very powerful formula.

This third book spotlights PRACTICAL APPLICATIONS of FENG SHUI - an easy to follow manual for those who wish to seriously utilise Feng Shui to enhance their luck and fortunes. This book addresses common problems faced by novice practitioners and provide answers to a broad range of common interpretative questions.

DEDICATION

*This book is dedicated to the memory
of my dearly beloved father
Lim Bor Yee
who left us on the first day of the lunar new year*

---

*and to my dearest family,
my daughter Jennifer,
my husband Wan Jin,
my mum, Nancy Lim,*

*for my brother Phillip,
and also
for all members of my extended family,
cousins, aunts, uncles,
in-laws, nephews, nieces ...*

Indeed No, I have not forgotten any of you

.... *about the* AUTHOR,

Feng Shui is Chinese geomancy, and Lillian Too's book on this centuries old Chinese practice is timely and topical... her book is convincing and thoroughly researched ... it is a beautiful effort at chronicling the many perspectives of Feng Shui ... it gives me great pleasure to recommend FENG SHUI to Malaysians and visitors alike ...

Y.B. Datuk Seri Dr. Ling Liong Sik
Malaysian Minister of Transport and President of the MCA.

" ... Lillian's research is a most welcome addition to the fast growing body of literature on FENG SHUI written in English".
Dr Ken Yeang. Phd (Cantab)
Architect & Environmentalist.

"Lillian Too's FENG SHUI is outstanding and spellbinding ... the well matched marriage between theory and practice contributes to the comprehensiveness of the book ... a reader's interest is sustained throughout the book, given the clear and precise style of writing, the effective illustrations and the interesting anecdotes... highly recommended ".
Dr. Leong Yin Ching, B.Econs. M.Educ.(Mal). Phd(Lon).
Professor of Education, University of Malaya.

"Highly readable ... and with interesting anecdotes "
Dr. Tarcissus Chin, CEO, MIM.

"A Masterful compilation" *Shahareen Kamalluddin*

... Lillian Too's book will provide the kind of information you need to keep the endless *chi* flowing into your homes or workplaces, and thwart the poisonous arrows of the *sha chi* which brings misfortune, il health and bad luck ... one could get hooked on the subject after reading Too's comprehensive book ... it provides an invaluable introduction to a subject that combines philosophy and conceptual principles extracted from ancient classical manuals ...
New Straits Times Book Review, (May 1993).

.... *Reviews on* FENG SHUI

CONTENTS

Opening Notes

PART ONE:
PRACTICAL APPLICATIONS OF FENG SHUI

Chapter 1
FENG SHUI of LOCATIONS   19

Chapter 2
FENG SHUI of HOUSES   44

Chapter 3
FENG SHUI of BUILDINGS & OFFICES   64

Chapter 4
FENG SHUI of APARTMENTS & CONDOMINIUMS 91

PART TWO
PRACTICAL WAYS TO IMPROVE FENG SHUI

Chapter 5
FENG SHUI ENHANCING TECHNIQUES   117

Chapter 6
FENG SHUI ENHANCING TOOLS   133

PART THREE
SPECIAL FENG SHUI APPLICATIONS

Chapter 7
FENG SHUI for CAREER SUCCESS 148

Chapter 8
FENG SHUI for BUSINESS SUCCESS 161

PART FOUR
SPECIAL TECHNIQUES & FORMULAS

Chapter 9
* EAST HOUSE WEST HOUSE
  THEORY of FENG SHUI 175

* EIGHT LOCATIONS
  THEORY of FENG SHUI 179

* PA-KUA LO-SHU
  FORMULA of FENG SHUI 188

* EIGHT LIFE SITUATIONS
  THEORY of FENG SHUI 194

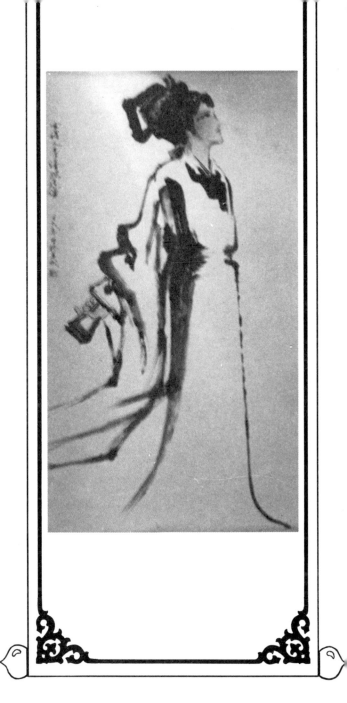

Opening Notes ....

.... *from the author*

This is my third book on Feng Shui. It is in direct response to the many requests I have had, for a book that deals completely with the practical applications of Feng Shui. Accordingly, to assist those who want to get the recommended procedures and guidelines as correct as possible, **this book focuses almost exclusively on application methods.** The situations showcased as examples, are illustrated with simple diagrams and sketches. The techniques highlighted for each situation are explicit, and presented in step by step sequences.

I have also addressed many recurring questions posed to me by readers, and those who have attended my talks and seminars on Feng Shui.

To begin with, a few words of advice are helpful. You will get more out of the practice of Feng Shui if you regard it as a science, and not as a religion. There are no spiritual connotations to the practice of Feng Shui. Only in so far as the underlying philosophy calls for balance and harmony with the earth's environment, does it demonstrate linkages to the mystiques of ancient Chinese cultural practice and belief.

The influence of superstitious beliefs and village folklore has imbued Feng Shui practice with localised dialect colourings. These originate from differences in interpretations.

In its long passage down through the centuries, meanings of symbols sometimes become associated with deities and other supernatural phenomena, so that over time, the mystical elements of Feng Shui has been equated with local spiritual and sometimes, religious doctrines.

Nevertheless, the philosophy and concepts of Feng Shui have more to do with complex mathematical compass calculations, and with the energy lines of the earth - colourfully referred to as dragon's breath or chi, than with faith in, or worship of any supernatural or divine entity. Understanding this enables the modern practitioner to accept that, contrary to popular belief, one is not required to believe fervently in Feng Shui's potency and power for it to work or not work. Faith is not a pre-requisite to success. Instead, effective creation of good chi flows, of balance and harmony are what are required.

It is necessary to analyse the methods, the suggestions, the techniques offered in particular situations. It is not necessary to endow the practice with faith or worship of any kind. Ask yourself - does what is suggested make good common sense.

Because Feng Shui really IS about good sound common sense. There is beautiful logic in the many explanations of symbolisms as well as in the various orientations, shapes and elevations suggested. The numerous "antidotes" offered to counter *bad chi and poison arrows* are also very logical. Much of Feng Shui has to do with conventional aesthetics, and with balance - too much or too little of anything - water, earth, fire, wood or gold is never advisable. As is so aptly symbolised by the Yin Yang emblem, good fortune can turn into bad fortune, and bad luck can also transform into good luck.

Feng Shui is also to do with achieving harmonious interface with the natural environment. Much of the rules and guidelines of Feng Shui reflect the importance of balance and harmony. And harmony is easy to achieve when the winds and the waters surrounding one's home does not conflict, or appear to be jarring, or hostile, or threatening.

Also, do not doubt the potency of subtle changes. Often times all that is needed is a shift of a few degrees in the placement of doors. A few inches difference in the dimensions of tables. A tree here, a plant there, a small pool or waterfall nearby, some light in a corner ... the objective is to create, and to attract happy vibrant chi.

To ensure it settles ... then will good luck enter your household, bringing prosperity & contentment, and a serenity to your family life.

Experiment. Monitor the results over a period of a few months. Become aware of the delicate transformations in your fortunes, and in your own behaviour. Is your family quarrelling less ? Are you achieving better communication between the members of your family and your colleagues. Has your luck improved ? Do you see fresh opportunities opening for you ? Has your income increased ? Is your business improving ? Are your children performing well at school ?

In short - are things getting better for you ?
Be honest with yourself. Guard against either imagined improvements or presumed worsening of circumstances.

Do remember that Feng Shui is not Magic. Its effects are not instantaneous. Manifestation of good luck is subtle and takes place over time. It is necessary to be patient, and to be wary of becoming too obsessed with results. Allow time for the chi currents to enter your home or office, and slowly attract harmony and balance into your life.

Sometimes when the Feng Shui "enhancer" used is too strong, you may feel yourself becoming more aggressive than usual - this is because the vibrations, or chi created are too powerful - if this is the case, make some changes. Perhaps your fishtank is too large, your plant too tall, your windchime too big - in relation to the size of your room. Remember balance is vital.

There are also many different *schools* of thought with regard to the practice of Feng Shui. Don't let conflicting advice confuse you unnecessarily. Or cause you distress. In essence, there are two main schools in Feng Shui, the landscape school and the compass school.

The landscape school focuses on the terrain of the land, the configuration of mountains, the flow of rivers, the shapes of land masses, the strength of the winds, the quality of waterways .... the techniques of landscape Feng Shui are very compelling !

Meanwhile, different branches of the Compass school offer different ways of identifying good and bad compass directions. These are in turn calculated from formulas using one's four pillars of destiny (the year, the month, the day and the hour of birth), which are then interpreted according to a variety of formulas, some based on element analysis, and others based on the Pa Kua trigrams and the Lo Shu magic square.

Much of Feng Shui practice is traced back to the premier influence of the ancient I Ching, and to the inter relationships between the five elements - water, wood, fire, metal, and earth. There are old texts available, containing explanations and dissertations on these ancient wisdoms. Their detailed study calls for much scholarship and effort. Interpretations of the ancient texts vary between scholars and Feng Shui Masters. It is hardly surprising then, that differences exist.

Happily, there are basic fundamental guidelines which every Master, and every Feng Shui text agree on. Where recommendations vary, the difference lies in different emphasis being placed on different components of Feng Shui practice or method.

Thus, some Masters maintain that good compass direction is more important than avoiding poison arrows ? Yet others argue over the method of discovering one's good directions ?

Then again, should Feng Shui practice be defensive or aggressive ie should we focus on guarding against bad chi or do we concentrate on activating and creating good chi ? Doing both is sometimes not possible, because for instance, the average household has only one main door, and we must decide which guideline to follow when confronted with two conflicting recommendations.

Are trees good or bad ?
Should one build a pool in one's compound ? How exactly does one describe the shape of one's home, especially when the shape is not exactly regular ? Do we consider the main entrance to an apartment block our main door, or is it the door to our apartment?

These and other equally practical questions abound.

This book explains the answers, using a variety of specific scenerios. Often there are important nuances and qualifications attached to recommendations given, and the novice practictioner would do well to pay close attention to the subtleties of the exercise.

Invest time and real effort. Invest time to understand, and invest effort to make any necessary changes. Understand the complex explanations of symbolisms that accompany recommendations you deem applicable to your particular situation. Track the results of changes made, and over time, you will begin to see and experience the benefits.

Over the years, I must confess I have greatly indulged my own interest in Feng Shui and have persistently sought explanations . I have also studiously investigated the results of Feng Shui features - to the extent that my observations of buildings, houses, rooms, offices and apartments, as well as their orientations is almost second nature. I am constantly on the lookout for the various manifestations of poison arrows which bring deadly poisonous and killing chi. And I am always looking around neighbourhoods, searching for dragon hills, for verdant lush vegetation, for slow, meandering and unpolluted waterways - and then investigating the general prosperity of the area.

Over the years my continious awareness of environmental Feng Shui has helped me check out things told to me by different Masters, and principles learned and extracted from interpretations of ancient manuals.

These investigations have strengthened my belief in the potency of Feng Shui, and heightened my awareness of the philosophies that underpin Feng Shui, so that the initial cynicism of the early years has now given way to a fervent, and beneficial belief. But it is a belief spawned of conviction rather than blind faith.

Nevertheless, I have consciously stopped myself from being too obsessed. I do not allow Feng Shui to rule my life. Whenever something I have tried does not work, I test out alternative methods.

And where it has not been possible to execute a Feng Shui inspired change to my home or apartment, I have almost always sought other methods - each time going back to the basics to understand precisely why the changes needed to be made in the first place. All the while trying to comprehend the true nature of the symbolic explanations.

Thus I continue to learn.

In recent years, the march of modern technology has further strengthened my belief in Feng Shui, because now I know ... now modern scientists have proven to me, beyond the shadow of a doubt that our atmosphere is crowded with many kinds of waves and energy flows, all vibrating at different rates - we have radio, television and radar signals just to name a few, which should convince us that the ancient concept of chi flows (the dragon's breath) must surely relate in some way to these atmospheric waves.

Signals that are invisible and yet are so powerful ! Similiarly, growing scientific investigations into human levels of consciousness - the beta, alpha, theta and delta levels, with their different speeds of brain wave activity must surely equate in some way to the chi flows of the human body referred to by the ancient Masters.

I offer you, my readers, no scientific answers to Feng Shui. Nor can I present definitive proof or documented evidence of Feng Shui's immense potency. But I do offer potentially rewarding food for thought. Plus suggestions on how you can attempt to vastly improve your luck through the practice of this very ancient Chinese wisdom.

Welcome Feng Shui's earth luck into your life.

It costs you nothing to try. Neither in terms of money, nor in terms of any significant compromise of religious or value systems. Look on Feng Shui as a science, an ancient wisdom that has survived the centuries.

It can bring you so much genuine good luck, so much peace and happiness. Surely an investigation into this incredible practice is worth some of your time and effort ?

Lillian Too
June 1994

PART ONE:
PRACTICAL APPLICATIONS OF FENG SHUI

Chapter 1
FENG SHUI of LOCATIONS

HOW TO SELECT GOOD FENG SHUI LOCATIONS

1. Begin your search for good Feng Shui locations by looking for gently undulating or hilly land, where the air smells good, where the winds blow gently, where clean waterways meander slowly, and where the surrounding vegetation is verdant and green. The nearby presence of elevated slopes, hills or mountains is a good sign, for these represent protection, and more importantly, symbolise the presence of the green dragon and the white tiger.

The ancient Feng Shui Masters of China understood that Man's destiny is enhanced when he lives in harmony with Nature, thereby tapping into its auspicious influences. Nature is likened to a living organism and its breath pervades everything, thereby producing varied conditions which modern practitioners term good and bad luck. The surrounding landscapes of one's home or workplace must reflect this harmonious interface with Nature for there to be good feng shui.

This harmonious interface with Nature is more easily achieved when the location of one's dwelling is situated in a place which taps into the auspicious influences of grounds and mountains, rivers and lakes; a place where the quality of the air and of the winds suggest an abundant presence of the good luck "breath" of Nature.

In Feng Shui tradition, auspicious locations are usually slightly elevated places where the green dragon of the East nestles gently with the white tiger of the West, with their bodies curving gently towards each other thus forming a horse shoe or an armchair shape; and is at the same time protected from the North winds by a range of hills that symbolise the black turtle ... while in the South, the presence of the vermillion phoenix considerably enhances the site. And if, facing this wonderful configuration of hills and mountains there is also a view of meandering or slow moving water; and if the vegetation in the area is green and luscious, then placing one's dwelling place here ensures an abundance of good fortune, of great comfort and of enormous wealth for the household for many succeeding generations.

For practical purposes, the would be practitioner must understand that all of these references to celestial animals is purely symbolic.

Dragons and tigers are in reality hills and mountains. Or contours of undulating land. As are also the turtle and the phoenix. In the modern context, practising Masters say that neighbouring buildings and houses can also represent dragons and tigers. It is, however, essential to note that the dragon "hills" must always be slightly higher than the tiger "hills". And that the dragon is to the left of you (or in the East) while the tiger is on your right (or in the West).

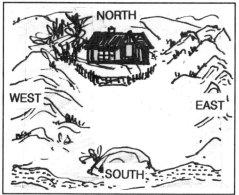

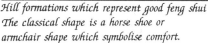

Hill formations which represent good feng shui The classical shape is a horse shoe or armchair shape which symbolise comfort.

The green dragon/white tiger formation

The breath referred to is the Dragon's cosmic breath, the *Chi* which plays such a central and pivotal role in the practice of Feng Shui - these are energy flows - invisible yet powerfully potent. Auspicious Chi is often referred to as *sheng chi. Feng Shui is all about capturing this chi, creating this chi and wherever possible, harnessing it into dwellings and work places.* Massive amounts of such auspicious chi exist in where dragon and tiger hill configurations resemble the sketches on this page. The search for good feng shui locations thus start with the search for the dragon. And where the dragon is found, there too will be the white tiger. Such places are NOT easy to find. The practitioner must use a little imagination. Here are some tips. Feng Shui masters advise that land that is completely flat cannot house dragons; nor can places where the air is "dead" and stale, where plants cannot flourish, where the soil is dry and lifeless, where the surrounding winds are harsh and threatening. Or where the shapes of hills are sharp and pointed. Dragons live by the sides of hillsides, never at the very peak.

Look for the dragon, and note the kind of landscapes to avoid !!

2. If you cannot find the perfect classical green dragon white tiger configuration, gently undulating land can also be auspicious. But pay special attention to the heights and distances of surrounding mountains. You don't want to be hemmed in by soaring mountain sides; nor be forced to site your front door facing a sharply inclined slope. Select a piece of land where you can orientate your home in a way that allows you a pleasant view, if possible, a view of meandering waterways, or of the distant sea. At any rate the view should be un-encumbered.

Where you can, try to locate a piece of land which allows you to design your house with its back protected by either a range of hills behind or where there appears to be support of some kind - a solid building, a clump of trees, or some form of gently elevated land. This represents the black turtle hills which "supports" you and your family through difficult times. It protects your back !

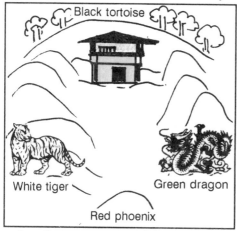

Shown here a representation of the classical ideal feng shui configuration, with dragon hills on the left and tiger hills on the right

It is important that any site you select should have some form of protection, and where it is not available, you must gauge whether you can "create" such protection artificially, for instance, by planting a row of trees. For this reason you should avoid buying land sited on ridges where there is a "drop" at the back of the house. This exposes you to danger. Where your land site is in an urban area, big buildings can also symbolise protection, provided these are not so huge (in comparison with your house) as to overwhelm you. Pervading all of Feng Shui is always the question of balance. Select the kind of land which allows you to design a balanced building or home, so that it merges naturally with the surrounding landscape or with neighbouring houses.

3. Look for land with compact, reddish loam. Such soil is full of the celestial breath of life or CHI. Avoid hard rocky soil where even grass cannot grow. In such places the feng shui is either dead or dying. When checking out a neighbourhood, observe how the plants and trees grow on neighbouring pieces of land; or in the immediate vicinity of your land. If the grass on your land is especially green and lush, it is a place of good feng shui.

If you are observant enough, you may sometimes find pieces of land which are "threatened by poison arrows", either it is facing a straight road, or a pointed roofline is aimed at it ... here the grass look sickly, brown or dry. Feng Shui masters believe that in areas where good sheng chi is destroyed by poison chi, even weeds cannot grow well.

On the other hand, where the accumulation of sheng chi is intact, the vegetation thrives. These spots where maximum amounts of sheng chi exist are usually more easily discernible in land which has not yet been developed. Often, when walking along a big piece of hilly or undulating land one can observe areas where vegetation thrives because there is balance in the amount of sunlight and shade (yin yang balance) and where there is a balance of moisture and wind.

Where hills have been cut for development purposes, and reddish soil is exposed, superstitious practitioners believe the exposed soil symbolise the dragon's blood; hence it represents an injured dragon which is bad feng shui. Until the situation is remedied with the replanting or re-growth of vegetation, it is advisable to avoid living in or near such locations. Thus, do not buy land with the intention of building your house immediately if your land is too close to areas still being developed, or worst still, when the hills being cut are just above your land. Injured dragons hovering above, create bad feng shui.

When selecting from plots of land which form part of an overall housing development, it is advisable to assess the entire area. If it is an area of good feng shui, the grass and the trees will easily grow again once the development is complete. And one of the best indications is the appearance and quality of the soil.
Fertile land is good feng shui. Dry, arid, rocky land is not.

4. Look for hill formations or sloping ledges that remind you of some good fortune symbol (eg a snake head or a dragon head, especially if appearing to be coughing out a pearl). If your land has a view of such a "symbol", living there will make you very rich. Three small peaks within view promise great academic honours for your children; while hills and boulders which represent malevolent or fierce animals (tiger, rat, eagle) could bring ill fortune in the form of bad health, or poor harvests.

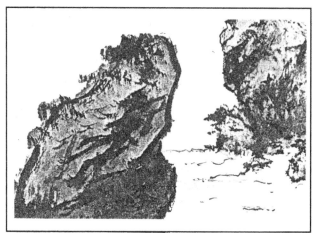

A rock formation is good
or bad depending on its shape

The practice of Feng Shui has always reflected the influence of symbols. And the spectrum of auspicious & inauspicious symbols is so broad as to leave room for the imagination to run riot. Hong Kong Feng Shui Masters are especially imaginative in their interpretations of rock, boulder, or hilly formations. If there is a noticeable rock formation, boulder or hill near land you are assessing; you are advised to gauge its impact. Try to imagine yourself confronting it each day as you move in and out of your home. If it "feels" threatening in some way, perhaps it is better to avoid it. On the other hand, if it makes you feel good each time you look at it, the energy flows from it may very well be positive. Wonderful stories abound in feng shui folklore of whole villages in China benefitting from a benevolent phoenix, or turtle rock watching benignly over the village's fortunes. Yet other stories relate how several seasons worth of wheat harvests were destroyed until a small hillock overlooking the village, and which represented a greedy rat was flattened. Do some proper research on *auspicious* symbols - they can be most helpful in your search for good feng shui locations.

5. Look for gently sloping hillsides that face water - the sea; a lake; or a mining pool. Water is usually associated with wealth and prosperity. But the water must be clean and should be ruffled by gentle breezes suggesting movement. Stagnant, polluted water create pernicious breath which brings bad luck.

The presence of water can also be artificially created; and this can be just as effective for feng shui. Where pools of water are man made, it's size and dimension should reflect balance and harmony. The nearer the water is to the land or dwelling place, the smaller its size should be, so as not to overwhelm the house with chi that is too strong. The further away it is, the larger the body of water can be.

Land that is nestled against hillsides, with a view of the sea in the distance is preferable to land which is too near the sea. The same reasoning can be applied to lakes and mining pools, particularly if they are large in size. Buildings with a view of water in front is excellent feng shui. Thus the use of the land being assessed also determines the nature of balance. Large buildings balance with large bodies of water, which may not be as suitable for bungalows.

Dirty water creates *sha chi* which brings unlucky vibrations, especially ill health for residents. It is worse if the water smells of decaying materials, or is muddy. It requires the presence of clean, free flowing water before wealth feng shui exists.

Land facing a small waterfall is auspicious

Land facing a peaceful lake is auspicious

6. Look for land where the balance of **YIN** and **YANG** is evident ie land which is neither too exposed to glaring sunlight nor too shaded by nearby hills; land which is not monotonously flat; nor too threateningly steep; land which is a combination of high ground and low ground; where rocks and greenery come together harmoniously; where it is not too damp nor too dry.

Balance is the most important word in feng shui.

Balance in Feng Shui refers to the presence of hard and soft; dark and light; yin and yang.

When applied to landscape feng shui it suggest a harmony of the various elements of nature - rocks, boulders, soil types, water and even the quality and type of vegetation.

When examining a piece of land, observe how these various elements coexist with one another. When they are in balance no single element overwhelms the others. Instead they complement each other and enhance the area's aesthetics substantially. In this context it is useful to examine the shapes of nearby hills. Check if they demonstrate various shapes that blend in naturally, one with the other. If possible, contemplate the way any proposed building of yours would fit into the land without upsetting feng shui balancing principles.

Avoid land which is too wet; to the extent that the place is prone to getting waterlogged. Also avoid land which is too dry to the extent that vegetation gets starved of water, and gets easily burnt by the sun. Too much sunlight is just as bad as having no sunlight at all. And too many hills is as bad as having no hills at all. Just as too much forestation is as bad as having no trees at all. Land must not be too YIN nor too YANG.

Balance at all times is the key to finding places with good feng shui.

7. Avoid locations on hilltops; in cul-de-sacs; facing a T road junction, or a straight line structure like transmission lines and railway tracks. These are areas most susceptible to being influenced by poisonous CHI which bring ill health and bad luck.

Land at the end of a cul-de-sac is not auspicious. Such locations suggest "no way out" when confronted with difficulties.

Hilltops rarely have good feng shui because such locations are susceptible to strong winds, and are exposed to the elements.

If you are fortunate enough to have a choice of land, it is advisable to avoid certain types of locations. Feng Shui Masters usually advise against purchasing land located at dead ends, especially if the land itself stands at the very end of the road. Not only does such land theoretically "face" a road coming straight at it, it also symbolically represents being placed in a tight corner. Particularly for people in business, living in cul-de-sacs suggest that when they are confronted with difficulties, solutions or escape routes will be hard to find.

Also avoid hill tops. These are inauspicious locations because water flows away from the land, symbolising a continious inability to amass wealth. There is also little protection against enemies as the land is totally exposed. If however, there is higher ground within view and one can locate one's home with one's back to the higher ground, the feng shui is considerably improved.

Also avoid land facing straight roads, railway tracks, and T junctions. These bring poison CHI which is difficult to correct. In feng shui anything straight that is pointed at the land or home is to be avoided.

8. Do not buy land that is hemmed in by two tall buildings, or land which faces, or is close to huge man made structures like transmission towers or water tanks. Also avoid locations which face buildings with crosses or steeples. These often create bad CHI which is difficult to combat.

In addition to the natural structures of one's surroundings, it is equally important to be very observant of other man made structures which can also bring inauspicious luck. Apart from unbalancing the CHI of the whole area, structures like transmission towers and large crosses (eg formed by two escalators or those placed at the top of places of worship) also direct poisonous CHI towards the land facing them.

Land that faces a building with a cross is inauspicious and should be avoided.

Land too near an electricity transmission tower could suffer from unbalanced CHI.

It is also not advisable living or working too close to such structures; Likewise, Feng Shui masters also do not like land that is situated too close to graveyards, cemetries, crematoriums and hospitals. These places emanate strong YIN vibrations that overwhelm the breath of life. Dragons are also seldom found near such buildings.

In the same way that hills which symbolise malevolent animals are to be avoided, man made buildings that resemble threatening objects or inauspicious characters are also to be avoided. Flyovers that look like knives and scythes "cutting" into one's land are also inauspicious.

Be wary of such structures and buildings, and scrupulously avoid buying land near or adjacent to, or worse, facing them.

9. Regular shaped land is always preferable to irregular shaped land, and the best shapes are either squares or rectangles. The shapes to avoid are the triangle, the L shape, and where parallel sides are of different dimensions. Irregular shaped land often imply that "some corner is missing", and the implications of this has to do with the eight sided Pa-Kua symbol where every side represents a favourable or auspicious life situation.

Although it is seldom easy to find regular shaped plots of land, it is wise to search for it because the basis for building a good feng shui house or building begins with a regular shaped plot. The eight sided Pa Kua and the Lo-Shu magic square, two vastly important tools of Feng Shui practice work best and easiest when applied to regular shaped plots of land. They are also more complete.

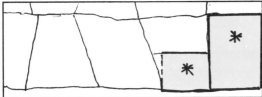

*The auspicious plots here are marked * and these can be observed to be regular shaped plots ie square or rectangular.*

These auspicious shapes lend themselves more easily to good feng shui designs because the Pa Kua and the Lo Shu magic square can be superimposed onto the land with little difficulty. Irregular shaped land, like the ones shown here, require various "cures"; and the Feng Shui of such land requires complex considerations. Thus, when purchasing land go for the regular shaped plots wherever possible. L shaped or T shaped land can be subdivided into two pieces of regular shaped land if large enough. Otherwise use lights to brighten "missing corners". Or plant some trees to camouflage the irregularity. Where one side of the land is larger than another side, enhance the narrower portion with lights.

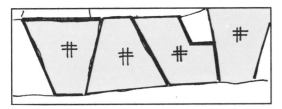

The inauspicious shapes are marked with a #. Avoid these shapes when buying land.

Good shapes are helpful, but don't sacrifice good chi areas for shape.

10. If you know your auspicious directions, look for land where you can orientate your main door to face your best direction. if you do not know your auspicious directions, look for land that preferably faces the direction SOUTH because many Feng Shui masters advocate this, based on the widely held belief that the south is the source of warmth and wealth.

You may investigate your exact auspicious directions from the LoShu PaKua formula contained in the author's second book on Feng Shui entitled, " Applied Feng Shui".

One of the most important elements of good feng shui is the orientation of the Main door. The Chinese have always regarded South as an auspicious direction, probably because in the China of the old days the North was always a source of biting north winds while the South gave out the promise of summer sunshine and good harvests. If you are familiar with the formula mentioned above, use it to determine the best direction of the master of the house (or the major breadwinner). Then let your main door face this direction.

There are many superstitious connotations attached to directions. Thus while the South is regarded as auspicious, the North is considered the source of ill winds. Some Feng Shui practitioners also maintain that an even worse direction is Northeast, because, they say, this is the direction to the gateway of hell, so that main doors oriented in this direction will recieve the pernicious breath of hell !!

The example given to support this was the orientation of the doors of the Hyatt Hotel in Singapore, whose subsequent re-orientation, it is claimed, led to a turning point in its business fortunes. The Hotel's business did subsequently improve, but the exact rationale for the re-orientation of its front doors has never been revealed.

Thus when purchasing land, make very sure you are able to position the main door of the house to be built, to face an auspicious direction, or better still to face YOUR auspicious direction.

Put some weight on this element of Feng Shui as main door orientations are very vital components in the search for good feng shui luck. It can make all the difference to one's fortunes.

11. Avoid locations which lie anywhere below or near the vicinity of a hill that has on top of it a boulder of large dimensions weighing heavily (and precariously) upon it. This kind of boulder above one's land could crush the fortunes of people living around the area, resulting in grave misfortune and poverty forever prevailing among them. Sometimes even an outcrop can be deemed to be similiarly threatening.

In Hong Kong during the sixties, a large condominium complex situated on the island's luxury Mid-levels area collapsed in the middle of the night, and rolled down the hillside killing over three hundred people. Feng Shui masters had repeatedly warned residents of imminent danger caused by an outcrop of rock located just above the condominium, one that resembled a malevolent frog with its mouth wide open, as if waiting to swallow up all those below. Those who moved out escaped the terrible fate of the residents who stayed on.

This is one of the most potent recommendations of Feng Shui Masters when assisting people to look for suitable land in hilly areas. While the search for dragons and tigers bring good feng shui, it is also vital to be always conscious of things that pose potential danger. Indeed, most Masters are agreed that even in areas which indicate good feng shui features, the presence of any natural structure or edifice that is pointed at or threatening to the

Never purchase land which appears threatened by a large outcrop or boulder above it. Here the outcrop resembles a rat. Bad !!

site negates everything. Good feng shui features CANNOT overcome the pernicious effect of such structures. Thus even where the auspicious horseshoe formation is found, where this is threatened by an intimidating rock outcrop, you are strongly advised not to purchase such land, unless you can somehow diffuse, deflect or destroy the threatening structure.

12. Examine the shape of surrounding hills to determine the various elements symbolised by each mound or elevated ground. Then determine that they are in harmony with each other; after which, select the land where there appears to be the greatest harmonious conjunctions according to the Productive and Destructive cycles of relationships between the elements.

It is vitally important that the elements represented by the configurations of the ground form a harmonious relationship. It is highly detrimental, for instance, if hills or boulders representing both fire and wood are in close proximity to homes as this renders the residents prone to quarrels and sufferings. On the other hand where the element combinations are beneficial, good luck prevails.

To practice this aspect of landscape Feng Shui, first learn to identify the elements associated with the different shapes of hills. Thus hills with sharp pointed peaks like these ∧ represent the element FIRE; Where the tops are gently rounded like this ⌒ the element represented is METAL or GOLD; if it rises steep and straight, and ends in a rounded or flat top like this ∩ the element represented is WOOD. Should the top resemble a plateau composed of soft earth like this ⌐⌐ the element represented is EARTH; And finally, if the plateau represented has an irregular surface with its contours resembling a lake or river, like this ⊂⊃ it represents the element WATER. When analysing shapes in this way, you will encounter variations and different combinations which may confuse you.

Very often even expert practitioners may not agree with each other on the element represented. There is thus a certain amount of instinctive recognition involved in the process of identification.

But there are other clues. Obviously soggy ground indicates the prevalence of the Water element, while barren rocks and boulders not cemented together with clay denotes Fire, while the abundant presence of trees denote a prevalence of the Wood element.

Take your time identifying the various elements present in the land, and try to get a feel for the more predominant ones represented.

The next step is to consider whether the elements you have identified are in harmonious relationship with each other; and secondly whether they are in harmonious relationship with your own element. Everyone's year of birth is "ruled" by one of the five elements. Check your own element from the tables given at the back of the book, and factor this in when making element assessments of your land.

To find out whether the elements are in harmonious relationship with each other, it is important to be familiar with the PRODUCTIVE and DESTRUCTIVE CYCLES summarised in the sketches shown below:

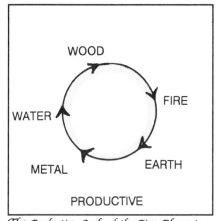

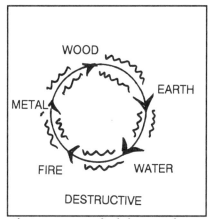

The Productive Cycle of the Five Elements   *The Destructive Cycle of the Five Elements*

From this information it is possible to discern auspicious and inauspicious combinations of landscape configurations. Additional guidelines on this aspect of element analysis are that: a large quantity prevails over a small quantity (hence water vanquishes fire); unsubstantiality prevails over substantiality (so fire conquers metal). hardness prevails over softness (and so metal destroys wood); density overpowers sparseness (thus wood consumes earth) and solid overcomes liquid (so earth vanquishes water).

It should be obvious that Man can intervene to improve the feng shui of a location by altering the natural configurations of the land. Hence, one can flatten a sharp pointed hill top and convert it from fire to wood, metal or any element so required ! Or even artificially create the type of land configuration deemed most beneficial from a feng shui viewpoint. Hence can feng shui be vastly improved.

13. Look for land that face waterways. The presence of slow moving rivers or gentle streams is always indicative of good feng shui. The best locations are those which seem to be "embraced" by water. So the auspicious CHI wraps around the house situated there, bringing good fortune to its residents.

To the Chinese feng shui man, water almost always symbolise wealth and prosperity. This is because water is believed to be excellent purveyors of CHI especially if they are slow moving, clean and meandering. This allows the CHI to settle, thereby bringing good luck.

Straight rivers, or fast moving waterways are not considered auspicious because the CHI is washed away even as it is created.

If your land is situated near a river, or even a little stream, it has exciting feng shui potential. Buy this kind of land. Just make very sure that the water can always be kept clean & unpolluted; and that the waterway never gets choked up, or blocked by garbage. This turns good luck into bad luck, and also brings illnesses.

And when you build your house make sure you orientate your home in a way which allows you to "tap" into the good CHI flows of the waterway ie that your main door has a clear and unencumbered view of the water flowing past the land and the house.

*Land located in areas marked * are auspicious.*

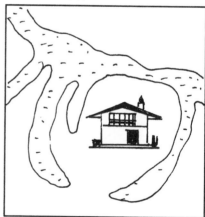

Being "embraced" by water is very auspicious

14. Analyse the elemental shapes of water courses to determine the relationships suggested. This allows you to gauge the extent of good luck you can enjoy from the river or stream near your land. As with hill shapes, the element relationships should be harmonious, and better still, blend with your own personal year element to produce extreme good fortune CHI for you.

When water courses meet or meander, the productive and destructive cycles of the elements also come into play. Thus, although water is, as a general rule extremely auspicious, the way the water courses meet is equally vital and important. Sometimes, certain configurations instead of bringing good luck, could very well bring misfortune. As when a fire shaped water; or a wood shaped water meet with a metal shaped water. This is because fire destroys metal, and metal destroys wood. Look at the elemental shapes of water courses below.

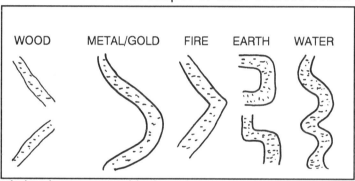

The five elements represented by shapes of water courses

To examine the relationship, see how two rivers meet, then convert them into their elements to discover whether the luck created is good or bad. The example shown here: a "water" stream entering a "metal" stream. Metal produces water, according to the Cycle of the elements, so the household living nearby can expect to enjoy prosperity and wealth for several generations. As with hills in a landscape, the shape of watercourses can be altered artificially to enhance feng shui. If you attempt to do this, ie to build water courses on your land, make sure you get your element relationships correct !!

15. It is also useful to consider advice given in the famous WATER DRAGON CLASSIC when assessing the relative merits of waterways near locations being considered. According to this Classic; ... *if water flows rapidly away from a site, it drains off - how can wealth and abundance accumulate ? If it comes in straight, and it goes off straight, surely it will injure Man ? ... Darting left, the eldest son meets with misfortune, and darting left, the youngest meets with calamity ...!!*

In the Water Dragon Classic, an ideal location is one that nestles among watercourses so it is protected in the belly of the dragon. Chi flows through watercourses and the branches that immediately surround a site and protect it are known as the inner Chi; whereas the main trunk of the river that surrounds the site at the outermost point carries the outer Chi; which has the ability to nourish the inner Chi, which in turn then penetrates the household. The sketches reproduced on this page show unfavourable locations vis-a-vis watercourses; while those shown on the next page indicate auspicious locations. In the sketches the black dot indicates the house/site.

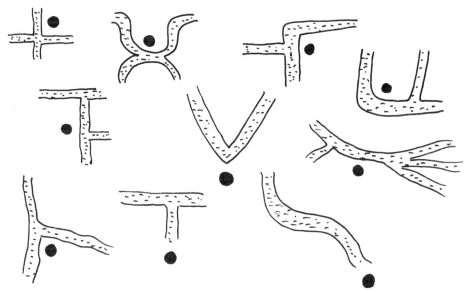

Unfavourable locations of sites vis-a-vis watercourses according to the WATER DRAGON CLASSIC.

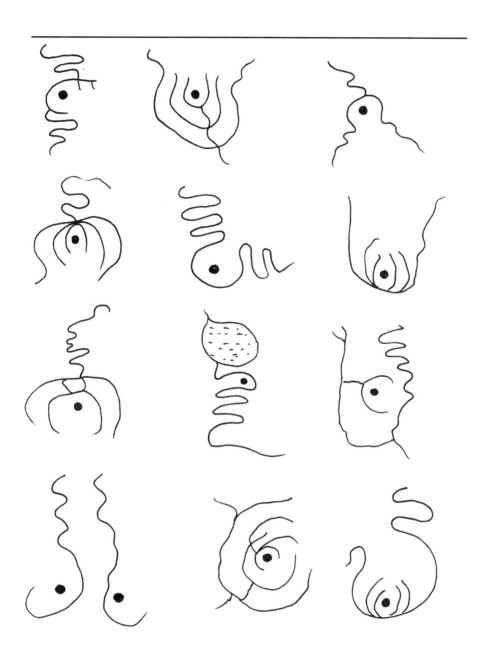

Favourable locations of sites vis-a-vis watercourses
according to the WATER DRAGON CLASSIC.
These are sites that indicate prosperity, wealth, fame and posterity.

16. Another useful source of good feng shui advice is the YELLOW EMPEROR'S DWELLING CLASSIC which says ... *a good earth will grow exuberant sprouts, a house with good fortune will bring prosperity.* According to this Classic, every site is affected by the spirit of the four celestial animals, which, even as you stand at your main door facing outwards, *you should see the green dragon is on your left, the white tiger is on your right; the black tortoise is at your back and the red phoenix is in front of you* ...

According to this fifth century classic, the colours of the four animals are linked with their elements. Thus the dragon is Wood; the tiger is Metal; the tortoise is Water; the Phoenix is Fire and in the centre is the house which is Earth. While these animals can be "identified" through the topography of the land dealt with earlier, it is also possible to identify them in watercourses. These are indicated in the sketches.

The DRAGON may be observed in a watercourse that has one bend branching off from the main river. A house/site located within this bend as shown here on the right (nestled in the stomach of the dragon) will bring wealth, honour and great happiness for many generations.

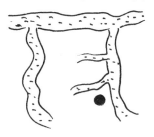

The TIGER is present in a river course with two or three branches. A house/site positioned in these branches, embraced by the Tiger's water promises great wealth, and great good fortune for many succeeding generations. Shown on the left.

The Tiger becomes malevolent and dangerous when two parrallel streams turn and branch out, and a house located between the two divergent courses is a tiger eating a corpse in its mouth. This symbolises bad feng shui - heralding poverty, death and an old age bereft of descendants to carry on the family name. Shown on the right.

The PHOENIX is present in watercourses which have sharp back turns, and sites located at these turns are inauspicious. Residents of such locations will be frequently troubled by hunger and poverty. The Classic also suggests that men who live in such places turn to dishonourable pursuits while women living here lose their virtue and honour easily.

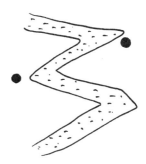

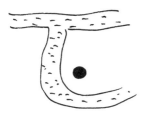

The TORTOISE is present in watercourses that show a loop caused by a tributary of the main river. Residents of sites located within this loop often enjoy high office and enjoy good family life which is blessed with many sons.

The IDEAL site (according to the Yellow Emperor's Dwelling Classic) is one that is surrounded by the green dragon water on the left; and balanced by a long flowing stream on the right representing the tiger - this stream must not be larger than the dragon water; nor can it encroach onto the left side because if it does, the dragon is unable to control it. This transforms the tiger into a harmful, malevolent presence. And in front, on slightly lower ground, there is a small pool or a lake representing the phoenix,

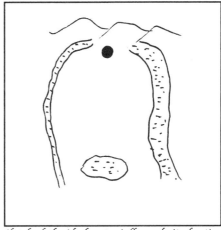

Sketch of the ideal water influenced site location based on the Yellow Emperor's Dwelling Classic

while behind, on slightly higher ground, a small range of hills representing the tortoise stand guard over the site. Such a location promises great wealth and great abundance for many generations.
It is important not to confuse this "water" interpretation of the green dragon/white tiger configuration with that of land masses (hills and elevated landforms) dealt with earlier.

17. When selecting small plots of land within special housing estates or developments, it is advisable to ensure that all the plots offered for sale are about the same size so that the houses that eventually get built will demonstrate a regular and balanced development, without the danger of the dimensions of any future house creating intimidating Chi for the rest of the neighbours. This encourages CHI to flow smoothly from one house to the next. Even better, if the developer places certain conditions which guard against this balance being unknowingly spoiled.

It is also advisable to investigate whether the land being offered for sale is reclaimed or filled land, since the earth CHI in such land is often unstable, and hence not very auspicious.

If the housing development include rows of link houses, or semi-detached houses which have been designed to face land plots you are considering, check the design of the facade of these houses to make sure you will not be hurt by pointed roof lines (poison arrows) when the houses eventually get built.

Also check the proposed internal road systems within the housing estate to ensure that any particular plot you are looking at is not inadvertently facing a straight road. You may not realise such a road is being planned until everything gets built.

Similarly, find out where the electricity substation and large water tanks are being located and try to avoid plots of land sited next to these structures. It is advisable to check on the width of future roads to ensure they are balanced in dimensions to the proposed houses to be built.

If the housing scheme comprise condominium developments as well, check that these multi storey buildings are not going to be directly facing your front door/gate. It could spoil your feng shui later on when they get built. Apartment blocks affect the feng shui of nearby houses in various ways, and the influence could well be inauspicious ! Finally, check the timing of construction of the phases of the development project so that freshly cut, exposed land do not adversely affect you

18. In the search for good feng shui locations, several texts refer one's attention to weather conditions prevailing on the day one goes out to view a piece of land. Be aware of the weather because it is believed that if it starts to rain even as you view the land, this is a sign that the land has good feng shui. However, if the rain develops into a major downpour or a storm, the day has become unbalanced. It is not a good sign.

It is important to stress that this particular piece of advise is as much based on superstition as on cultural folklore. The Chinese have always believed that some light rain falling is an auspicious sign for almost anything - as it signifies a happy sky dragon frolicking in happiness. In Feng Shui, because water signifies money, light rain is therefore seen as a good luck sign.

Along the same vein, it is also pertinent to mention that most Feng Shui Masters are extremely particular about the time of the day when they are asked to investigate sites or homes for purposes of Feng Shui. They believe that at certain hours of the day, it is inauspicious for them to view land.

The author is unable to offer definitive times of the day when it is best or worst, to view land since Feng Shui masters differ in their opinions on the matter. However the general concencus seems to be that the early hours of the morning, just after sunrise is considered a good time to investigate sites. And that it is preferable not to view land in the evening, when the sun is on the wane. This, they say is because you want to see how the rising sun affects, or shines on your site, in order for you to assess the mix and balance of yin and yang.

The sun and sunlight is yang, while shade and darkness is yin. When the sun rises, one is able to gauge the impact of yang on the yin of the land which prevailed through the night. If the balance is good, one gets a good feeling about the land. And if it is unbalanced the feelings generated are believed to be discordant, and hence inauspicious. In countries where seasonal changes in weather affect outdoor investigation of land sites, the advice is to do it at midday hours in winters, and at sunrise hours in the summers.

SUMMARY OF WHAT TO AVOID IN LOCATIONS.

Avoid land at the summit of hills or elevated ground. Such locations are areas of dangerous chi, being unprotected and vulnerable to the elements.

Avoid land which directly face poison arrows, be they natural or man-made; like this house here which faces the sharp edge of the building opposite. Bad chi, bringing misfortune, has been created.

Avoid land which faces a T junction. This kind of straight road pointing at the site is bad feng shui. In fact, anything straight or sharp pointed at a site is to be avoided at all costs.

Avoid land which is directly opposite another house (or building) whose sharp, triangular roof line is aimed directly at your site. This type of poison arrow is difficult to deflect.

SUMMARY OF WHAT TO LOOK FOR IN LOCATIONS.

Look for land which is surrounded on three sides by undulating or hilly land; with the land on the left side slightly higher than land on the right side.

Look for land which is protected at the back by slightly elevated land, or by a clump of trees which serve to deflect ill fated Chi.

Look for land which has a view of water in the distance. If you live on slightly elevated land and your home is oriented to face the sea, it is generally regarded as very good feng shui.

Look for land that is embraced by auspicious waterways and make sure you then orientate your main door such that the water flows past it, and you have an unencumbered view.

Chapter 2
FENG SHUI of HOUSES

HOW TO BUILD A GOOD FENG SHUI HOME

19. To build a home conducive to good feng shui, start by designing a house with a REGULAR SHAPE. Squares and rectangles are far superior to houses which have "protruding" extensions; or which are L-shaped; U-shaped or which are narrower in some parts than others. Regular shaped houses are deemed to be balanced and complete, and lend themselves more easily to feng shui enhancement.

Avoid triangular shaped houses, or houses that have too many corners. The angles created give off unfortunate *sha chi* and are not conducive to the attraction of good CHI flows.

In the same way L-shaped houses are also to be avoided because this shape resembles a meat cleaver and is inauspicious. In addition L shapes suggest missing corners, thereby creating imbalance.

Another unlucky configuration is the U-shaped house. Residents living in such homes suffer from unhappy marriages, and will be plagued with frequent quarrels. There is a great deal of unhappiness.

Irregular shapes caused by extensions to the main house either to house garages or kitchens, or extra rooms are also not advised. As far as possible stick to the rectangle or even better, the square shape, and make certain that corners do not have double protrusions.

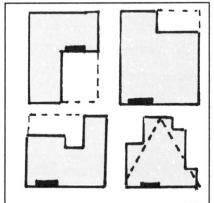

The L shape; the U shape; the triangle - these are the inauspicious shapes to avoid. In addition, house shapes which have protrusions and double corners should also be avoided.

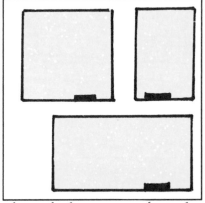

These regular shapes - squares and rectangles - are more conducive to good feng shui. They are also easier for various feng shui enhancers to be designed into the home later.

20. Plan the Siting of the house carefully. Do not place the house too far in front, nor too far behind when "placing" it onto your land plot. The ideal is to site the house in a way which allow balanced dimensions to be maintained. So neither the front garden nor the backyard is disproportionately large or small.

Do make certain that the house is sited to get sufficient sunlight. Observe the impact of sunlight on your land, and ensure a good balance of shade and sunlight - yin and yang.

If there is room for a driveway, it is important to make the driveway even in width throughout. If the driveway is straight make sure it does not end directly pointing at the front door of the house. If it does, it becomes a poison arrow, and the effect is worse if the driveway gets narrower as it approaches the house. Circular driveways are best.

If the land on which a house is to be built is odd shaped, use garden lights to enhance narrow corners thereby "regularising" the overall shape. A common problem with small land plots in housing estates is that the house to be built is often too big, leaving insufficient room for gardens. In such cases, enhance the corners of the land with lights.

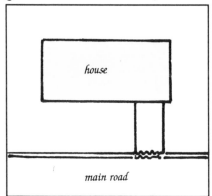

Site the house in the centre of the land, so that front garden dimensions and backyards are well balanced. Keep driveways even in width.

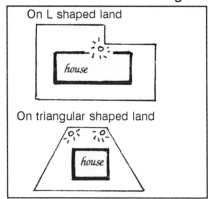

In odd shaped land, try maintaining balance by locating the house in the centre. But install lights at the corners of narrow or missing ends.

21. Design a DRIVEWAY that is friendly and non threatening. Circular driveways are the most conducive to attracting good luck CHI flows, as Chi moves in a circular fashion. Curved driveways are also preferable to straight driveways.

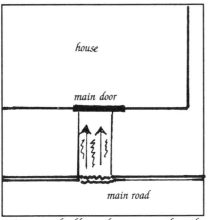

Driveways should not be narrower than the main door. Nor should it be straight and pointing directly at the front door. BAD !

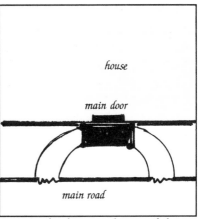

Semi circular driveways bring good fortune. Circular driveways are also auspicious.

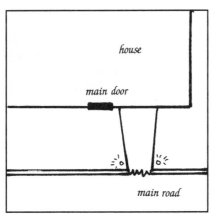

Driveways which narrow out (shown here) or which narrow in, have a limiting effect on business/financial opportunities. Also bad for careers. Lights at the narrow ends help.

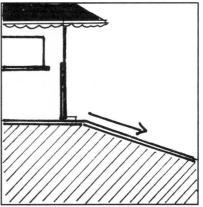

Driveways should not slope downwards away from the house. Chi flows out, draining away money luck. They should be broad and level.

22. Before starting construction, check and double check your house ORIENTATIONS Make sure your house (and its main door) are facing your best, most auspicious directions, and be very exact in your measurements ! If you do not know your most favourable directions please refer to the formulas & theories in Chapter 9. Or if you prefer, you may also follow the advice laid out in the YANG DWELLING CLASSIC which advise that main doors be sited to face the direction SOUTH ...

The YANG DWELLING CLASSIC which is much favoured by Feng Shui Masters is a Manual which lays down certain guidelines on house and room orientations. According to this Classic, the most important rooms in the house eg the master bedroom and the study room, as well as the main door to the house should face SOUTH.

Kitchens, it says, should face EAST; and never SOUTHWEST. The elder members of the family should sleep facing SOUTHEAST. And if the family is doing business, then its business premises should also face SOUTH and never NORTHEAST or SOUTHWEST.

Because there are several methods of determining the best compass orientations to follow, practitioners would do well to check out various methods before deciding the direction best suited to them. Chapter 9 contains two excellent methods for consideration; the East House West House method, much favoured by Hong Kong Masters because this is based on an analysis of elements; and the Pa-Kua Lo-Shu formula which the author has found to be extremely potent.

The orientation of the MAIN DOOR has a crucial and pivotal role in determing the excellence of one's feng shui. This is because the main door is considered the entry point of CHI into a household. It should therefore be oriented to attract good chi. More, its direction should benefit the Master of the household; so if there are several people living in the same house, the main door must be oriented according to the birth date of the Master of the House.

The main door must also be protected against being hit by poison arrows which create bad shar Chi.

23. Protect your MAIN DOOR from poison arrows. This is one of the most crucial aspects of Feng Shui practice. Even if the rest of your house has excellent feng shui features, a poison arrow hitting at your main door negates everything. This rule takes precedence over compass directions. If there is a sharp angle or a massive structure facing you front door, you MUST re-orientate it even if it is your best, most auspicious direction !!

The negative effects of secret, poison arrows is so dreadful that Feng Shui Masters always look out for these arrows first when asked to investigate the feng shui of a house. And to ensure you do not have this problem, you need to be aware of it when buying land or selecting a house before you commit yourself.

Many different things, natural and man made, can constitute poison arrows. Some are more obvious than others. The practice of feng shui involves the need to be alert to these arrows; and this requires the development of one's powers of observation.

What are these poison arrows and how do they work ?

Basically, anything sharp, angled, or pointed, or straight, contain secret poison arrows, and when directed at your front door, they cause misfortune -ill health, loss of opportunities, severe difficulties in business, quarrels, a continious series of problems, loss of money. Poison arrows create *sha chi,* lyrically referred to in the old texts as pernicious, noxious breath, the antithesis to *sheng chi,* the cosmic breath. Under this category are angled rooflines; straight roads, railway lines, a tall tree, telephone poles, steetlight poles, crosses, towers, the edges of neighbouring houses or buildings, a ridge of hills, straight rivers or canals, drains ... in fact the list is not exhaustive.

In addition, front doors should also not open to a solid wall or other obstructions, like retaining walls, flyovers, a steep hillside, an overpowering building, a huge water tank, a transmission tower, or other massive structure. These too, create sha chi. The MAIN DOOR must not face any of these structures.
Be defensive. Protect your main door !

SOME EXAMPLES OF POISON ARROWS

A single tree is a poison arrow

A single tree facing your front door could cause havoc in your family life by blocking good chi from entering your home. If it is on your own land, cut it down. If it is outside, and you cannot do anything about it, you may have to reorientate your main door. Please note: if there are several trees in a clump, they do not constitute poison arrows - only a single tree whose trunk appears threatening is a poison arrow.

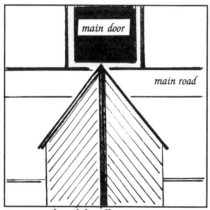

A steep and angled roofline is a poison arrow

A steep angled roofline facing your front door brings severe bad luck, causing illness amongst children and family members, and even worse, creating problems for your career and business. Angled roofs are most severe when the angles are sharpest because sha chi created is powerful. The best solution when you are building your house is to reorientate your door so that the effects of the bad chi are deflected away from it.

A cross ...

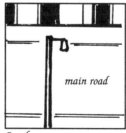

A pole ...

Edge of a flyover ...

THE MAIN DOOR: *Summary of Feng Shui tips*

* The main door should be properly installed and its dimensions must balance with the rest of the house. If too large, it could cause financial difficulties and if too small, it will create discord within the family.

* Place your main Door towards the left hand side, the green dragon side, so the dragon can exert his energetic spirit over your house. You may also place your main door in the centre, but unless your most auspicious direction is on the right hand side, you should try to avoid the white tiger side of your house. Take directions from inside the house.

* The main door should never face directly onto a Y shaped road or path as shown in the sketch here. This symbolises difficult decisions and misfortune within the family, in business or at work.

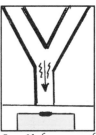

A Y-shape road facing the main door is bad feng shui

* The main door should never face directly onto churches, temples, monasteries, or cemetries. These places exude massive quantities of YIN and will thus create imbalance. It is alright if these religious buildings/cemetries are at the back/side of the house.

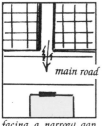

facing a narrow gap between two buildings is bad feng shui

* The main door should never face a narrow gap between two buildings. This causes the family savings to be squandered away. Small back-lanes, situated between two buildings and facing one's main door directly also cause poor health and business loss.

* The main door should never directly face a mountain or hillside. This could result on extensive business losses and work difficulties. Orientate your door such that the hillside protects your side or back, rather than cause you difficulty.

* The main door should never directly face a bend in the road, a bend in a river, or the edge of a flyover. This symbolises the house being cut by a knife or blade - symbolising acute health and financial problems.

* The main door should not face anything straight, or sharp or massive. It should also not face a dead end, a garbage heap or a clogged drain!

24. When designing your house, give adequate consideration to the notion of BALANCE. Good feng shui is all about creating and maintaining balance between the various elements of the environment. This means keeping an eye on relative dimensions of the house itself to the surrounding environment; the size of doors and windows, the size of rooms, the number of doors and windows; it means keeping a balance of sunny and shady areas, of greenery and concrete, of colours and of yin and yang.

Balance creates harmony, which in turn creates good sheng chi for the house. if your house is so large as to overwhelm the neighbourhood, and worse still, overpower your land, make sure you have compensating features designed into the house plan. The use of garden lights has the effect of "extending" the garden, while colour schemes can be used to balance out the "yang" force of a house that is too big. Select yin colours (ie dark colours).

Balance should also be reflected in the ratio of windows to doors (3:1); in the size and height of rooms. Large airy rooms are better than small rooms, but they should not be so large, nor so high as to overwhelm the balance. If possible let the elements represented by colours, timber, bricks and other building materials be harmonious by checking the element relationships and their productive/destructive cycles. Symmetry is preferred to asymmetry.

If possible, adopt a house design that does the least "damage" to your neighbours houses (ie from a feng shui perspective).

Do not design huge angled roof lines that hurt others because they may adopt feng shui "cures" (dealt with in later chapters) which may hurt you. Let your rooflines reflect a hill shape which represents an auspicious element. If in doubt, design roofs which are not too sharply angled. Feng Shui masters usually advise against the fire element roof line ie $\wedge \wedge$ for obvious reasons. A cluster of mildly undulating roof lines are often recommended, ie those which suggest Wood or Gold ie $\cap$ or $\frown$.
Finally balance should be maintained by landscaping the exteriors of the house. Provide for this in your plans.

25. Houses must have auspicious LAYOUT plans to create good feng shui for various members of the household. There are specific methods for allocating different corners of the house to different members of the family. There are also various feng shui guidelines for the different function rooms - bedrooms, kitchens, dining rooms, toilets - the doors, corridors, corners, beams, levels, staircases, and their relationship to each other.

The first step to designing house layout is to identify the various "corners" of the house based on the eight sided PaKua symbol. This exercise will result in there being nine different sectors identified ie the eight outer corners plus the centre. Each of the sectors correspond to one of the compass directions, either the primary directions, north, south, east and west or one of the secondary directions, northeast, southeast, north west and southwest. This is shown in the diagram here.

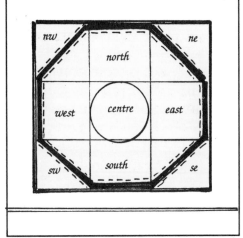

The first step in house layout design is to segment the house into nine sectors corresponding to the eight compass directions and a centre. This identifies the nine "corners" or "sectors" of the house.

With this working diagram, you can then proceed to the next step, which is to superimpose the PaKua symbol onto the houseplan (drawn in dotted lines in the diagram above). Obviously if you have two levels in your house - upstairs and downstairs - the same dimensions and corners will apply to both levels. Your design of rooms in the two levels can then be based on how you want to allocate the different corners.

Depending on which method you wish to use - and there are several methods summarised in Chapter 9 · you will then be able to identify the corners/sectors best suited to each member of your household. You can also identify the wealth and other corners of your house as well as the most suitable locations for the different function rooms.

There are two main methods which can be used to allocate rooms in house layouts. These are:

1. THE LIFE SITUATIONS METHOD.

This is based on a well tried method popular in Hong Kong which identifies various life situations for each of the eight compass corners of the PaKua symbol. The eight life situations and their matching directions, together with suggested function rooms are summarised as follows:

* **WEALTH** is represented by the Southeast (Study, Office).
* **FAME** is represented by the South (Study, workrooms).
* **MARRIAGE** is represented by the Southwest (daughters rooms).
* **CHILDREN** is represented by the West (children's rooms).
* **MENTORS** is represented by the Northwest (children's rooms).
* **CAREER** is represented by the North (children's rooms).
* **KNOWLEDGE** is represented by the Northeast (children's study).
* **FAMILY** is represented by the East (master bedroom)

There are many uses of the Life Situations Method of Feng Shui but for the purposes of layout considerations, a knowledge of the significance of each corner enables the practitioner to allocate sectors more efficiently.

2. THE PAKUA TRIGRAMS METHOD.

The PaKua symbol has eight different trigrams arranged around its corners and these also symbolise various members of the family. You can also be guided by the Trigrams when arranging house layout. Thus:

* CHIEN placed NW represents the father.
* KUN placed SW represents the mother.
* CHEN placed East represents the eldest son.
* SUN placed SE represents the eldest daughter.
* KAN placed North represents the middle son.
* LI placed South represents the middle daughter
* KEN placed NE represents the youngest son
* TUI placed West represnts the youngest daughter

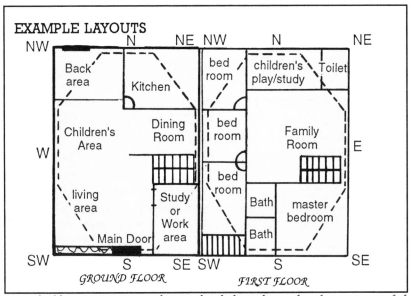

Example of layout arrangement with rooms identified according to the Life Situations method.

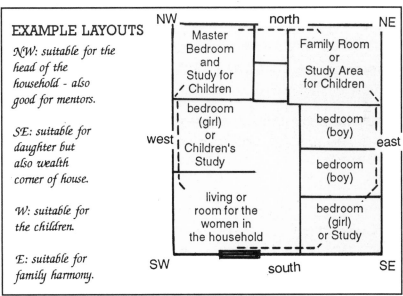

Example of house layout, with room arrangements made according to the PAKUA Trigrams method. It is also possible to combine both methods, thereby getting the best of both methods.

26. There are some general Feng Shui guidelines which should be incorporated into layout designs. These suggestions, if properly implemented during construction, will generally guard the household against misfortune, ill health, petty burglary ... In addition they generate a harmonious flow of CHI within the home, thereby contributing to family goodwill and happiness.

DOORS: Do not have three doors in a row, especially if one of them is a back door and one is a front door. This is most inauspicious.
DOORS: When there are doors facing each other, make sure they are of the same width and height, and that they face each other directly.
DOORS: When two doors are at right angle to each other make sure they each open and shut into the rooms concerned.

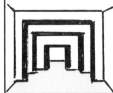

BAD: 3 doors in a row

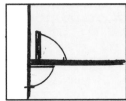

BAD:clumsy doors

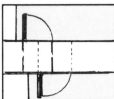

BAD Unbalanced doors

CORRIDORS: It is preferable not to have long corridors at all in a residential abode since these represent straight arrows that create sha chi. If there are too many doors leading off the corridor, it also causes quarrels and rifts between family members. At the same time, the room with the door at the end of the corridor will suffer from bad sha chi created by the long corridor.

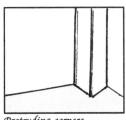

Protruding corners are bad feng shui

CORNERS: should be kept to a minimum; and all protruding corners should be eliminated from the house plan as these create sharp poison arrows which hurt residents. Too many corners also cause lost opportunities and cause residents to suffer from frequent headaches. Where possible corners should be decorated with plants, and they should be well lighted as these encourage CHI to settle and circulate.

OVERHEAD BEAMS: There should not be any exposed overhead beams, especially heavy structural beams in the main areas of the house, of the kind illustrated here. Sitting or sleeping under such exposed beams cause stress and ill fortune. The advice is for these beams to be covered with ceilings or

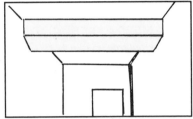

BAD: Exposed overhead beams

camouflaged in some way. For those who use plaster ceilings, please take care that the designs chosen do not include corners or angles. Owners should explain this important consideration to over enthusiastic interior decorators.

COLUMNS: Feng Shui practitioners often warn against having stand alone columns in the home, especially if these are square columns. Bad structural design sometimes is the cause of such columns becoming necessary. The four corners of the column give off poison chi, and wherever columns are required, the advice is to make them round or to wrap them with mirrors. Use a tall plant to camouflage the corners.

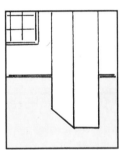

BAD: Square columns in the house which must be camouflaged.

SPLIT LEVELS: are not generally encouraged, but if you have designed your ground floor to have split levels make sure your dining area is located on the higher level. This ensures that the CHI of the residents is higher than those of visitors, who are entertained in the lower level living room. Bedrooms and family rooms and studies, should never be located on the lower levels of a house for the same reason.

STAIRCASES: should never start directly in front of the main door, nor end directly in front of an upstairs door. The CHI then created is too strong and hence becomes harmful. Staircases should ideally be curved gently, rather than straight. Spiral staircases resemble corkscrews and are not recommended, especially when placed in the wealth corners of the house. Staircases should not be too narrow or too steep. And the steps should always be covered; not exposed.

27. The clever use of MIRRORS within residential abodes can produce beneficial feng shui for its residents. Use mirrors to enhance your feng shui, BUT also be aware of the bad effects which mirrors can create if placed wrongly.

Mirrors are extremely useful feng shui tools. They can be used to deflect poison arrows; to "extend" tight corners or "missing" sectors; to activate the CHI flows in certain rooms and also to camouflage sharp angles caused by columns. But there are certain rules which must be observed when you use mirrors.

Wall mirrors can be used to reflect good luck symbols into the house.

Mirror walls are excellent for the dining area because it is believed that the doubling of food on the dining table symbolises abundance for the household. Such mirrors should not be too low as to have the effect of "cutting" off the heads of the tallest residents; These mirrors should also not be reflecting the main door or any other door that opens to the outside. This has the effect of symbolising CHI flowing in, and then out of the house.

Mirrors are also excellent for reflecting good luck symbols & beautiful scenery of water, rivers or lakes. This brings wealth into the house.

Mirrors can also be used to wrap around square columns to dissolve bad CHI surrounding the four sharp corners. They can also be used to "extend" out walls thereby balancing incomplete house shapes. Mirrors should not reflect staircases; doors; stoves or toilets.

Feng Shui masters also warn against mirrors in bedrooms because the CHI created is too powerful for the resting person. Where they are present in the bedroom, make certain they do not face the bed !

28. Design the shapes of rooms with care. If possible make all your rooms REGULAR in shape, ie square or rectangular. Avoid triangular or L shaped rooms because these create inauspicious results for the inhabitant. Where there are adjuncts to the rooms eg. adjoining dressing areas and toilets, make each of the rooms regular in shape. Where built-in cupboards are installed, make certain these do not cause imbalance by leaving small gaps or tiny corners where sha chi can accumulate.

It is much easier to create balance and harmony when rooms are regular in shape and dimension. For those who are fastidious, they can also take the trouble to make sure dimensions of all rooms represent auspicious feng shui measurements (*feng shui dimensions are given in the author's second book, "Applied Feng Shui"*) although this is not absolutely necessary.

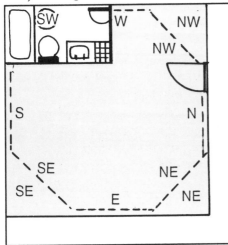

The PaKua superimposed on an L shaped bedroom. Note how the attached toilet caused the L shape, and also note that the toilet is in the marriage corner!

However, do avoid having odd-shaped rooms, or rooms with sloping ceilings. They are terribly inauspicious. L shaped rooms for instance symbolise a meat cleaver and unless you are sleeping in the area which represents the handle (ie the short part) you will suffer from misfortune. L shaped rooms are also deemed "incomplete" when you attempt to superimpose a PaKua onto the room layout, and depending on the orientation of the room, the missing corner could well represent one of the things you want eg your Career, or Wealth, or Marriage prospects. Indeed, it is possible to use the PaKua's life situations to identify the significance of every corner of one's room. In the example given here, the bedroom has become L shaped because of the attached bathroom. If you note the compass directions of the superimposed PaKua, you will see that the marriage corner houses the toilet. Such an arrangement will cause marriage prospects to be flushed down the toilet ! The same analysis can be made for other situations represented, eg. wealth, career, family and so forth can be similarly affected.

29. When designing your house, try to tuck away the TOILETS. Feng Shui always recommend that this particular room be made as inconspicious as possible. Definately the main door should not open too near to the toilet. Nor should staircases and dining rooms face toilets. Within the toilets, let the WC be hidden from obvious view.

One of the strongest recommendations made by Feng Shui masters is that toilets should never be conspicious. And most definately once you have identified the wealth or career sectors of your house you should guard against locating your toilets in these sectors. These are the SE and North sectors of your home. The effect of locating toilets in auspicious sectors is that you will be flushing away all the prospects of that sector's luck. Hence if any of the other sectors represent situations important to you (eg fame, family, marriage) you would do well to make sure toilets are not sited in those sectors.

You should also not locate toilets in the middle of the house as this spreads the bad vibrations all round the house. Instead toilets should be sited along the sides of the house.

TOILETS should also not be too large, so that for those who wish to install luxurious bathrooms into their homes, make sure the WC area is nicely tucked away in a corner of the bathroom, and if possible, half walled up so it is not visible from the wash basin area. Shutting it away from view deflects the sha chi created.

TOILETS should not be located in the vicinity of the main door since the excess YIN created by the toilet will clash severely with the YANG coming through the front door into the house.

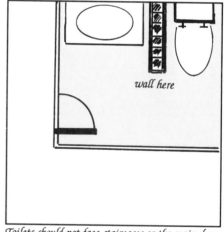

Toilets should not face staircases or the main door. Shown here: an example of toilet location which does not harm the household. The WC is half walled up so it is not visible from the basin area.

30. The KITCHEN is sometimes regarded as the source of treasure for the household. As such kitchen doors should not be facing either the front door or the back door, otherwise the good luck could slowly leak out of the house. The orientation of the STOVE is also extremely important. Hence kitchen design must take this factor into consideration.

Feng Shui Masters believe that when Kitchens and Stoves are placed in auspicious locations and are facing good directions, the result for the household will be extreme good fortune - wealth, abundance and high positions of honour. According to the YANG DWELLING CLASSIC, the most ideal location for the kitchen is the East or South, but never the Southwest sector of the house. Also, the element Fire is linked with the South and the element Wood is linked with the East. Directions symbolising wood and fire are thus appropriate for the kitchen, or cooking area.

While it is advisable to locate the auspicious sectors, it is also necessary to take note that the cooking area must NOT directly face the main door. This creates severe bad luck for the household. Also, the kitchen door should NOT face the living room area as this causes ill health and worse, sow discord amongst family members thereby leading to arguments and quarrels. You must thus adjust accordingly.

Within the cooking area special consideration should also be given to the exact location of the Stove or cooker. This should not be too near the wash basin as water and fire will clash !

And even more important is the direction of what is referred to as the "fire mouth". The fire mouth should face one's auspicious direction, *so that that one's food is cooked with the energy that flows from one's lucky direction.* In modern rice cookers the fire mouth is the plug that fits into the pot. For gas cookers, it is necessary to look for the place where the gas flows into the cooker. Design your kitchen to take this into account. Practitioners of Compass Feng Shui strongly believe that if one's fire mouth direction is incorrect, severe bad luck will prevail. Since different members of the family have different auspicious directions, it is advisable to have two rice cookers in the family !

31. What about SWIMMING POOLS ? Modern Feng Shui Masters are mixed in their recommendations. One group vehemently opposes the idea of having swimming pools altogether, gleefully pointing to various examples of family fortunes lost by the second generation and attributing the cause to the presence of large swimming pools in the house. Another group of Masters maintain that pools can be auspicious if they are nicely balanced with the house and the land; if they are sited correctly on the land and if they are curved in shape, embracing the house, instead of rectangular and having sharp corners.

Since Feng Shui precepts warn against sharp corners, it stands to reason that rectangular pools of water are inauspicious, especially if they are too large. The CHI created would be too strong if the house itself seems overwhelmed or dominated by the pool.

But Feng Shui guidelines and philosophy also pronounce at great length about the auspicious influences of water. It therefore seems logical to accept that man -made bodies of water, if designed to blend harmoniously with the environment should be auspicious, especially since many Masters maintain that the good luck features of the WATER DRAGON CLASSIC can be artifically built to benefit households. The author believes

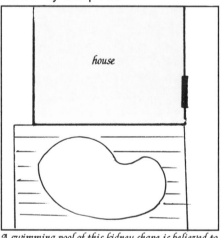

A swimming pool of this kidney shape is believed to create beneficial Chi to the residents.

that water IS auspicious, because it represents wealth. More so if the water element is deemed good for you, according to your horoscope. However, swimming pools should be round, or curved or kidney shaped if you wish to have one in your house. And do make sure that its dimensions do not overwhelm the rest of the house or site. Maintain balance, and include plenty of landscaping so that the pool blends in naturally with your garden.

32. If you build EXTENSIONS to your house, you must consider the effect these extensions have on the overall shape of your house. It is important to note that certain shape combinations are auspicious while others are inauspicious. At the same time, examine the element of the extension based on where it is located ie which of the driectional sector it occupies and then check its impact on the element represented by your main door.

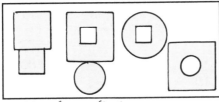

Auspicious shape combinations

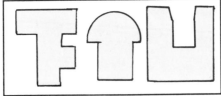

Inauspicious shape combinations

Reproduced here are some examples of auspicious and inauspicious combinations.
At the same time you can also be very imaginative and design auspicious shape combinations of your own that are based on lucky symbols & characters.

Another method of determining the feng shui effects of extensions is to use the element analysis of the direction of the extension. Thus if the extension is built on the northern side of the horse, it represents the element water. If the main door is located facing the southeast (which represents small wood) then the extension will enhance the door's feng shui since Water produces Wood. On the other hand if the extension is located in the northwest, representing big metal, then the extension will have a detrimental effect on the door since Metal destroys Wood. This method of analysis is highly recommended since element analysis is one of the fundamental principles of Feng Shui practice. These corresponding symbols may be gleaned from the diagram of the PaKua reproduced at the back of the book.
This same analysis can be applied to the building of gazebos, stand alone garages and other significant sized structures planned for the garden. The effect on the main door should be ascertained because so much of the feng shui luck of one's home is centred around the feng shui characteristics of the main door

Chapter 3
FENG SHUI of BUILDINGS & OFFICES

33. All the basic principles of feng shui that apply to the building of a home also apply to the designing of an office. Harmony and balance are important concepts which, when applied to the place of work will promote an environment of cooperative goodwill, that enhances productivity, and, more important, attract auspicious good fortune for the businesses and companies housed in these workplaces.

Office feng shui refers to the feng shui of interiors - how offices should be laid out; design features to be incorporated into the plan, as well as features to be avoided; the dimensions and shapes of the various rooms; the orientations of the managers' offices; the arrangement of desks and furniture; the flow of traffic in large open areas; the doors and entrances to the office and the most ideal locations for the different departments.

In addition office feng shui should stress features and orientations which promote good interpersonal relationship between employees; between colleagues, and between bosses and subordinates. If offices suffer from the pernicious effect of bad sha chi, incessant arguments, constant bickerings and a great deal of counter productive politicking could very well result. There would also be continious health problems leading to illnesses and high levels of absenteeism amongst staff.

Thus while the principles of feng shui may be similiar, practical considerations suggest that the areas of emphasis will surely differ. Office harmony, and the promotion of excellent productivity are what are normally aimed for in the design of good feng shui offices.

Also, modern offices are usually housed in multi storey buildings of at least three levels, and are often located in busy town centres. These characteristics also suggest a different set of applicable guidelines from those recommended for residential houses or even apartments.

Office feng shui thus focus on work, on business luck, on career luck and on achieving high turnover, clear thinking, good management, and a cooperative work force.

34. Start by checking the feng shui of the office building which houses your office. Look out for poison arrows, obstacles and inauspicious orientations. Check the characteristics of nearby roads, traffic directions and neighbouring buildings. And search for auspicious features like rivers, waterways, and landscaping.

The poison arrow in the form of a cannon placed in the opposite building for aesthetic reasons is pointed only upto the fifth floor of this building

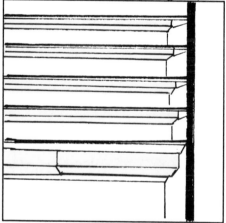

Structural beams get repeated floor after floor thereby affecting those on the lower floors more severely than those on the upper floors.

Often when buildings suffer from inauspicious orientations, or when an offending poison arrow is pointed at a building, all offices within the entire building are adversely affected, although sometimes not to the same degree. Shown here on the left is a building threatened by a cannon aimed at its building entrance. Its pernicious effect is felt, but less and less as one goes higher. Offices housed on the lower floors are more affected by the cannon those those on the higher floors.

The effect on lower floors can also get magnified eg exposed structural beams which offend feng shui concepts are felt to a much greater extent by the lower floors in a multi storey building since structural beams on every floor above will be "pressing" much more on the unfortunate person sitting below the beam on the lower floor. There will be so many beams pressing him then !

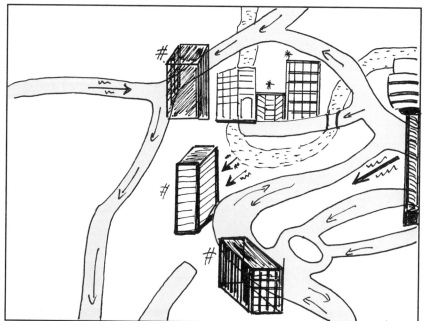

Examine the general area around the office building. In the layout map above the buildings which could be affected by poison arrows are marked #, while auspicious buildings are marked *.

It is always a good idea to study the general appearance of roads and buildings located around your office building. Examine the flow of rivers and traffic; the shapes and size of neigbouring buildings - their height and dimensions. If you are hemmed in by two buildings larger and taller than yours it is not very auspicious.

When there is a harmonious balance between buildings, the CHI flows in an auspicious way bringing general well being and prosperity to everyone. Every straight road, sharp angle, or the edge of other buildings is a potential threat so be on the lookout for these. On the other hand buildings gently embraced by roads enjoy good feng shui; as do buildings which face a park or gardens. Trees at the back of a building represent protection while buildings on the left hand side should be slightly higher than buildings on the right hand side, thereby simulating the green dragon white tiger configuration.
If the land your building stands on is irregular in shape, make sure there are lights placed at the irregular corners to simulate balance.

35. When assessing the APPROACH ROADS to an office building, it is useful to observe the directions of traffic flow. T junctions are bad, but if there are several roads leading obliquely towards the building, and these are inclined gently downwards towards the building, it is believed to be very good feng shui since water and lucky CHI are flowing towards the building. But if the incline is too steep, the CHI becomes too strong and is then inauspicious.

Buildings which face a roundabout are also believed to enjoy good feng shui as the traffic brings circulating CHI flows towards the building. The effect is especially auspicious when several roads are connected to the roundabout. Flyovers however are not auspicious, as these are viewed as "threatening" towards a building. Sometimes the unlucky CHI is so serious it is better to move out. Flyovers resemble sharp knives cutting into the belly of a building.

In the same way, buildings that face roads which form a cross in front of it are inauspicious. This is a serious feng shui defect, which can however, be countered by planting a clump of trees to block off a view of the roads. When assessing buildings therefore, try to remember all the guidelines dealt with so far. Thus, buildings facing Y junctions and T junctions are to be scrupulously avoided.

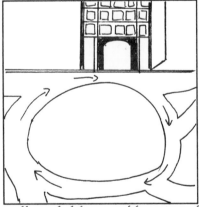

Buildings which face a roundabout enjoy good feng shui, but if there is a flyover nearby, it is bad

Buildings which face a crisscross of highways may suffer from bad CHI emanating from it

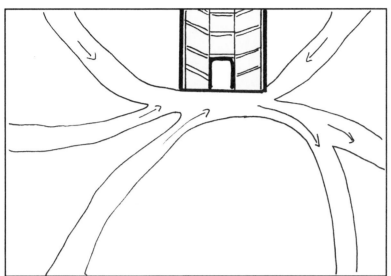

A building which has several roads converging opon it, as shown above is hurt by the roads coming at it (in front), but the roads coming from behind bring good luck. In such situations, most masters believe the effect is generally ausppicious especially if the roads slope gently downwards towards the building. Where the slope is steep however, the CHI created is too strong and thus becomes inauspicious. The traffic flow is also important.

Examples of buildings which have auspicious and inauspicious feng shui. When assessing buildings, be very observant about traffic flows.

A building which faces a Y junction is inauspicious and is best avoided.

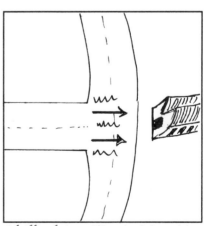

A building facing a T junction is inauspicious

SOME EXAMPLES OF HARMFUL LOCATIONS FOR BUILDINGS

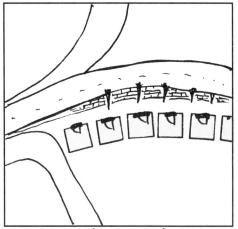

An inauspicious configuration caused by a new flyover blocking the main door.

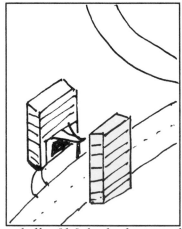

A building "hit" by the sharp pointed roof design opposite.

Buildings that are smaller, and lower than surrounding buildings will be adversly affected

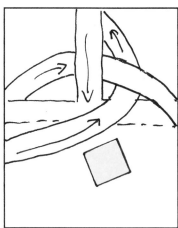

This building was orientated to avoid the bad chi coming from the opposite road but is now affected by new flyovers

MORE EXAMPLES OF HARMFUL LOCATIONS FOR BUILDINGS

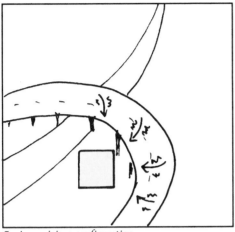

*An inauspicious configuration
caused by a hostile, cutting flyover.*

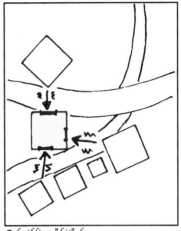

*A building "hit" by
various neighbouring buildings*

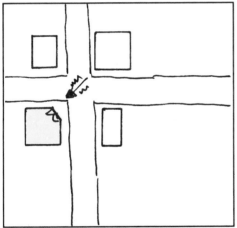

*Buildings at junctions are seldom auspicious.
Note the corners of buildings affecting each other.*

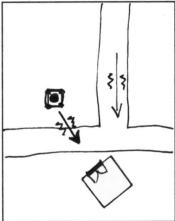

*This building was orientated to avoid the
bad chi coming from the opposite road
but is now affected by the tall tower
being built.*

THE BANK OF CHINA BUILDING IN HONG KONG

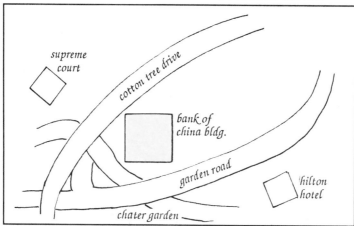

The surrounding roads around the Bank of China Building in Hong Kong

When the Bank of China Building was first completed, its prismatic facade which comprised crosses and angles caused much concern amongst feng shui watchers in Hong Kong. Many felt the building had bad feng shui, and that its many angles would cause problems for other buildings in the vicinity. Since then however, several Feng Shui masters have studied the building, some using sophisticated advanced methods of calculations based on the building's orientations and its "natal chart". The concensus has been that the building actually enjoys very auspicious feng shui.

Look at the sketch above. Note the concentration of benevolent forces. The building is located in an area of busy traffic flow, and several flyovers on Cotton Tree Drive and Garden Road cross the front and back of the building. In Feng Shui terms, roads and flyovers are like rivers, and usually if the curves of a flyover bends towards a building, it is likened to a blade or a scythe cutting into the building bringing inauspicious Chi. But look carefully again at the curves. In actual fact, the curves do NOT cut into the building. Rather these curves "embrace" the building, and resemble a river meandering slowly round it. Why ? Because traffic lights on the roads slow down the traffic, thereby ensuring that Chi approaching the building does not dissipate. The flyovers therefore represent a benevolent configuration bringing good fortune to the building. Expressed lyrically and in classical terms, the building may be described as being " *saluted and hugged by multiple rivers with love and affection*". Further more, directly in front of the building is an empty space represented by Chater Garden which symbolise the place of favourable Chi accumulation. Again an auspicious feng shui indicator.

THE HSBC BUILDING in HONG KONG

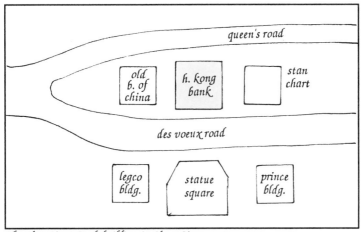

The HongKong Bank building in Hong Kong

The Hong Kong Bank building in Hong Kong was always regarded as being closely allied to the economic fortunes of this British colony. There are countless stories surrounding the two stone lions that guard the building. And about the feng shui of the building itself. It was widely believed that the excellent feng shui of the Hong Kong Bank building in previous decades had contributed greatly to the prosperity of the colony. Thus when the decsion was made to demolish the old building in 1981 and to replace it with a new building, Hong Kong residents - who are all great believers of the importance of feng shui - voiced their concern, some even drawing co relations between the massive collapse of the stock market in 1982/83 to the period when the new bank building was being constructed.

When this new and present building was finally completed at a phenomenal cost, and then inaugurated in July 1985, the colony's Feng Shui Masters examined its natal chart and the physical surroundings in detail before pronouncing their approval. Based on both numerology LoShu based calculations and its physical surroundings the building is auspicious.

Look at the sketch above. Besides sitting on an auspicious dragon location, it also has Statue Square in front of it, a place where Chi gathers and accumulates. Victoria harbour and the star ferry nearby also help in accumulating the Chi in the area.

Meanwhile, the buildings next to it - the StanChart Building, Princes Building, the Legco Building and the old Bank of China building act as dragons and tigers to form a most auspicious configuration. Traffic from Des Voeux road flows slowly at a slight incline bringing good Chi as well.

36. Whether or not a building is auspicious or inauspicious depends to a very large extent on the feng shui characteristics of its main entrance. This must be in balance with the building itself, and should preferably face lucky directions. The rules which govern the determination of orientations for houses generally apply to buildings as well. If the building belongs to your company, orientate it to suit your horoscope or that of your boss. If you are renting office space within the building, use the guidelines on general orientation, which recommend facing South for good luck. Another lucky orientation is South East which represents wealth.

Yet another way of determining whether the entrance of a particular building suits you (and therefore will be good for your business) is to use element analysis. According to the PaKua arrangement of trigrams based on the Later Heaven Arrangement, each of the eight directions correspond to one of the five elements:

* South = Fire   * North = Water
* East = Big Wood   * West = Small metal
* Southwest = Big earth   * Southeast = Small wood
* Northwest = Big metal   * Northeast = Small earth

Now check this against your own ruling element (based on your year of birth - found in the tables at the back of this book).

Next analyse whether the main entrance direction belongs to an element which will destroy your element (*Fire destroys metal which destroys wood which destroys earth which destroys water which destroys fire*); and also whether it exhausts you (*Fire exhausts wood which exhausts water which exhausts metal which exhausts earth which exhausts fire*). If it falls into either of these categories, the building is unsuitable for you. Locate elsewhere.

On the other hand if the element of the main entrance belongs to an element that produces and enhances your element (*Fire produces earth which produces metal which produces water which produces wood which produces fire*), then the CHI of the building is in harmony with your CHI. It is suitable for you.

37. Please remember that the best approach to the practice of Feng Shui is to be as scientific as possible. The general guidelines given so far, have been extracted from ancient texts, but they have also been adapted to suit a modern environment. Also, it is not always possible to exactly follow these guidelines, especially when confronted with other dictates of the landscape school of feng shui, like avoiding poison arrows. Other times, factors which have to do with unusual horoscope configurations can also affect one's suitable directions. These are based on very complex compass school calculations which are quite beyond the scope of the average person. As such, the best approach is always to be very aware of subtle changes to your well being and to your business when you first move office, or after you have made feng shui inspired changes. This kind of conscious monitoring increases your awareness of fundemental principles, which in turn will make your efforts more successful

Also consider: Very advanced feng shui, as practised by the Hong Kong Masters are based on difficult formulas and calculations which take various things into consideration, eg the general luck of the year, its ruling elements, its auspicious numbers and so forth.

At the same time, there is also the 20 year period of luck, and auspicious numbers to consider. These calculations have a subtle bearing on the "luck quotient" of certain directions and certain numbers based on the Lo Shu magic square of numbers. A chapter on some of these more complex methods is included in this book, for those who wish to investigate further, and be even more exact.

For others who may not wish to pursue the more sophisticated calculations and formulas, guidelines of the landscape feng shui system are perfectly adequate to ensure that your physical abode and work place does not make you vulnerable to bad CHI.

It is far more practical to guard against poison arrows and avoid potentially damaging locations, than it is to attempt practising and implementing the very precise applications of the other schools.

38. The next step in designing a good feng shui office is to select space which leads harmoniously off the lifts and escalators. This affects the feng shui of the main entrance door to your office. Avoid some of the more common mistakes illustrated here; and ensure that your office layout design takes note of the features to be wary of, and to avoid.

This office main door directly faces an escalator which in turn faces the building's main entrance. Bad feng shui. Luck seeps out.

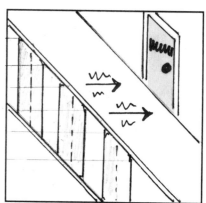

This office main door directly faces a bank of lifts. Not recommended.

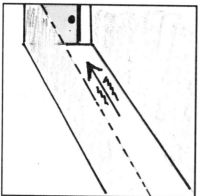

Do not locate your office main door at the end of a long corridor which acts like a poison arrow. Your business will be badly hurt.

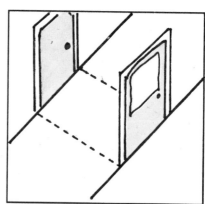

If your main office door faces another door make sure the doors align perfectly, otherwise you will quarrel with your neighbour.

39. From the inside looking out, the **MAIN DOOR** should preferably face a direction that suits the boss of the office ie based on his year of birth and using the PaKua LoShu formula summarised at the back of the book. In addition there are some useful tips on main doors which can be easily implemented.

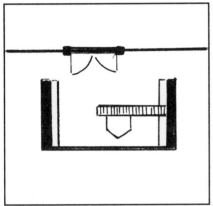

The foyer area should not be too cramped. If it is, use mirrors to enlarge the feeling of space. Mirrors should not directly face the entrance.

Make sure the foyer is well lighted. Poor lighting causes CHI to stagnate or die.

If there is a receptionist stationed at the foyer, she should avoid facing the door directly.

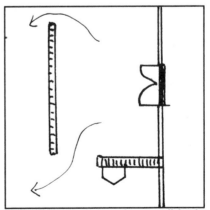

It is always a good idea to have a wall divider in the foyer which conceals the inside office.

40. OFFICE LAYOUTS should be designed to facilitate the auspicious flow of CHI. Long corridors should be avoided, and placement of dividers and desks should ensure that sharp corners do not face any one. Place plants to supplement dividers as these provide good balance. The office should be welllighted, and traffic flow should meander rather than sharply aligned.

In the sample layout shown below, several positive features can be noted. The placement of dividers and desks are balanced, and are conducive to attracting good feng shui. Office layouts are important for ensuring harmony in the work place. Generally doors facing each other should be aligned directly facing each other or there could be many disagreements. Too many doors also has the same effect. Meanwhile, open plan offices are conducive to good feng shui so long as the desks are not "hurting" each other with sharp angles.

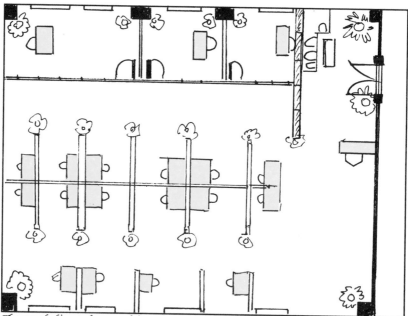

The sample layout shows good feng shui features. No stand alone columns to block Chi flows. Protruding corners are camouflaged. The main door is screened from view.

41. PROTRUDING CORNERS are regarded as inauspicious structures. They are compared to sharp knives or hostile fingers pointing directly at the person they hit. These corners can also be hitting at important filing cabinets, or be facing the door of the manager's office. There are several ways to dissolve the bad CHI of such corners and these are highlighted here.

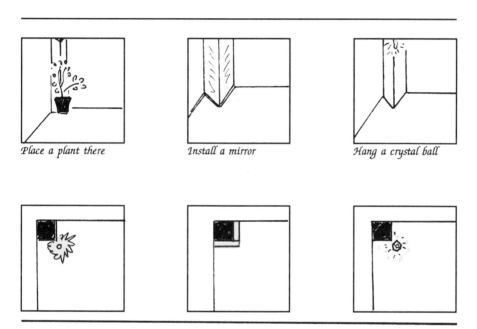

Place a plant there   *Install a mirror*   *Hang a crystal ball*

When getting your office designed make sure you incorporate these little feng shui features to take care of projecting corners.

Hanging a mirror on one or both side of the corner has the effect of making it "disappear".

Or you can place a strategic leafy plant (an artificial one will do) at the corner to soften its edges.

Or you may also hang a faceted crystal ball from the corner. This dissolves bad Chi coming out of the corner and effectively shields the occupants of the room. if you have several corners like these in the office it is a good idea to vary the treatment recommended.

42. All EXPOSED BEAMS and stand alone COLUMNS in the office must be attended to. Beams are believed to have a very oppressive effect on those who sit near it, or worse, directly under it. The same goes for those sitting at the edge of square heavy columns. The bad CHI created is also harmful to the office as a whole.

The best way to deal with exposed beams in the office is to totally camouflage it with false ceilings, but even then do take note of where they are and try not to place desks or chairs directly under it. Another method is to use the symbolic PaKua method. Hang two flutes which have been dressed with red thread on the offending beam. They should be hung facing each other with the playing mouthpiece at the bottom, thus resembling the sides of a PaKua. Yet another method is to try and camouflage the beam with creeping plants. Beams in confined and small rooms, or in hallways are particularly harmful.

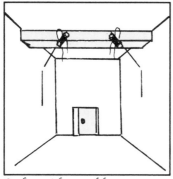

Dealing with exposed beams

Such beams resemble blockages which will severely affect the flow of CHI within the office. Where the beams appear in a manager's room, they should be treated immediately otherwise, his entire department might suffer.

Beams also affect creativity and cause headaches. Try to keep them hidden !

As for columns, square ones cause much feng shui harm.

Round ones are acceptable.

Square ones have to be wrapped with mirrors, or the corners softened by using creepers and plants.

This has the effect of dissolving bad Chi and serves as a protection for the person seated nearby.

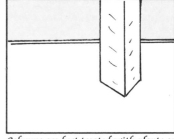

Columns are best treated with plants or mirrors

43. The MANAGER or DIRECTOR'S room should ideally be located deep inside the office, but not at the end of a long corridor. The fortunes of the office are influenced by the feng shui of the boss's office. If you are the boss, do make sure your room follows certain feng shui guidelines if you wish to enjoy good luck in the office.

Offices designed according to feng shui principles attract career and business luck to the occupant.
There are several guidelines which you can follow. Thus:

* Regular shaped rooms are better than irregular shaped rooms.
* If your office room is L shaped use mirrors or lights to counter the bad Chi flow. Mirrors should be wall mirrors.
* If there are projecting corners or beams or columns in your room, treat them with feng shui features accordingly.
* If the window opens out to a view of a poison arrow, keep the window permanently shut.
* Do not build book shelves on the wall facing you. The shelves act as knives cutting at you.
* If you have a sofa set in your office make sure it is not arranged in a way which has a corner of the arrangement pointed directly at you.
* Check your ruling element and identify the element which "produces" your element, and then suitable symbolic objects to enhance your element. Thus if wood is good for you, place a plant; if fire is good for you, put a bright light or something red like a painting; if water is good for you place a small fish tank; if metal is good for you place a small windchime in a corner; and if earth is good for you place a natural quartze crystal on your desk.
* Design your colour scheme also according to your elements. Thus green for wood; red for fire; black or blue for water; yellow for earth and white for metal.
* Check the best direction for your door. Use the formula given at the back of the book ie the PaKua LoShu formula.
* Finally, make certain that nothing is hurting your door. Look at the office space just outside your office. Ensure that nothing pointed or straight is aimed directly at your door. If there is camouglage it with plants.

44. Correct desk placement plays a large part in enhancing office feng shui. There are several guidelines which you should try to observe. Examine these in detail.

* Never sit with your back to the door. You could be betrayed or be "stabbed" in the back by a colleague.
* Never sit with your back to the window. You will symbolically be lacking in support. If the window is permanently covered it is OK.
* Try to sit facing the door, at whatever angle you like, but make sure none of the corners are cutting at you.
* Check your best seating direction from the PaKua LoShu formula, then align your desk accordingly.

GOOD DESK PLACEMENTS

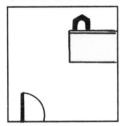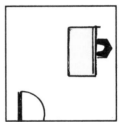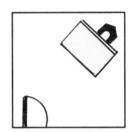

BAD DESK PLACEMENTS

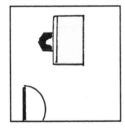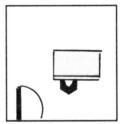

Whatever your seating arrangement do make sure it does not seem awkward. Do not attempt to sit facing your best direction and in the process get "stabbed" by poison arrows or end up with your back to the door.

In feng shui it is better to be defensive first before trying to enhance your luck. Even if you are unable to tap your best orientation, it is better to follow the guidelines given above.

45. The location of your OFFICE and its relationship to the whole office can also be examined. There are auspicious and inauspicious placements depending where it is vis a vis the main door; what its shape is and where the manager actually sits.

In addition to the way your desk is positioned, also take a look at your office, be it a room or an office created by modern office dividers. Once again the golden rule about not having your back to the door applies; nor should your office be too near the main entrance. If your office has a glass partition wall, do make sure it does not directly face the entrance, and avoid irregular or L shaped, or slanting offices.

GOOD OFFICE LOCATIONS

In the opposite corner

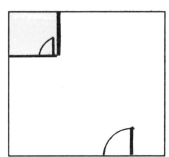

Tucked auspiciously at the far end

INAUSPICIOUS OFFICE LOCATIONS

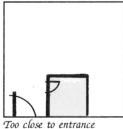

Too close to entrance

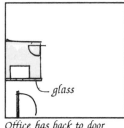

glass

Office has back to door

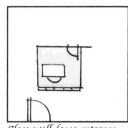

Glass wall faces entrance

46. If you have no choice and have to deal with an IRREGULAR shaped office, it helps to introduce certain feng shui cures or antidotes to counter the bad vibes created by the odd shapes. With irregular shaped offices you can use lights to "regularise the shape and also position your desk carefully.

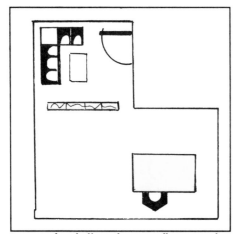

In an L shaped office, place a small screen, and sit facing the door as shown in the sketch above.

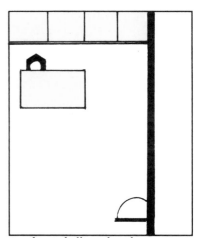

An elongated office whose door location is fixed - cupboards can "shorten" the office.

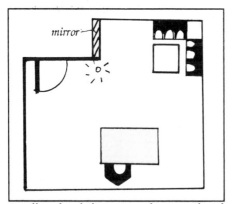

An office shaped this way can be corrected with mirrors on one wall, and have a light at the corner. beware the poison arrow of the corner !

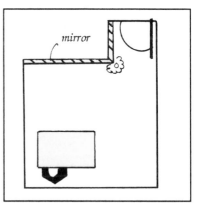

This office can be improved with a mirror. Note seating position.

47. When designing BOARDROOMS, do not ignore the standard guidelines about angled corners and overhead beams. But also protect the chairman's seating placement. This should preferably be away from the entrance, with his back properly supported by a solid wall. Do not have too many doors opening to the board room, as it leads to quarrels and misunderstandings and is not conducive to harmony.

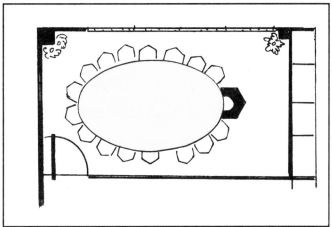

Example of a good boardroom arrangement. The chairman's seat is away from the door, and supported by a a wall. The room is a regular shape. Corners are camouflaged.

The boardroom layout shown here has no obvious feng shui defects. Since board rooms are where important negotiations take place it is not a bad idea for bosses to position their sitting direction to face their most auspicious direction, as indicated by the PaKua LoShu formula. This ensures they will have valuable feng shui luck each time they chair a meeting or an important negotiation. It is also a good idea to find out what their best LoShu sectors are and then position the board room in their best, most auspicious sectors. This ensures that the boardroom becomes a source of luck for them. Another useful feng shui tip on boardrooms is to examine which element is best for the chairman, or person who regularly uses the room. This is obtained by checking one's ruling element in the year of birth. If water is good for you, install a fish tank for luck, designing its location in a way which merges with the decor. If fire is the element which brings you luck, use red as part of your decor; if wood is good for you, incorporate plenty of plants, if metal, use a windchime and so on.

48. Viewed from the inside of the office, there are certain things to avoid and certain guidelines to follow when positioning the MAIN DOOR and other doors within the office.

The main door of an office should never open directly facing into a toilet. It should also not face another door directly, as this forms a straight line causing Chi to move too swiftly through the office.

The main door should also not face an open window, since this encourages the vital Chi to fly out the window. This same rule applies to the back door of the office as well. If there are interconnecting doors within the office these should preferably not be placed in a straight line, but should rather "meander" through the office.

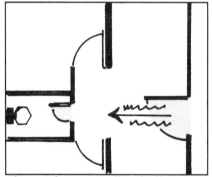

The main door into an office should not face a toilet.

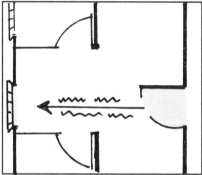

The main door should not face a window, or the back door.

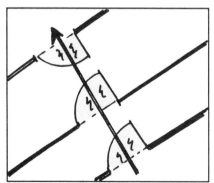

Doors within an office should not be designed in a straight line

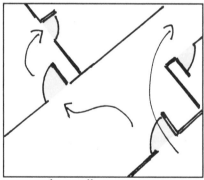

Doors within an office should "meander" through as shown.

49. According to the PaKua Eight Situations School of Feng Shui, the room housing the big boss or the Chief Financial officer should be placed in the sector of the office symbolising the wealth/prosperity sector which is the SOUTHEAST sector. This encourages wealth luck for the office. The human resources or personnel manager should be placed in the EAST sector to promote family and cooperation amongst employees and staff.

Research staff should be placed in the NORTHEAST while young trainees or new staff should be placed in the NORTH or WEST sectors of the office. These relevant sectors are believed to govern various aspects of good feng shui particularly suited to the different job functions within a company. Obviously much depends on the nature of business which an office is engaged in. Thus if the business is stockbroking, the dealers and traders should be in the Southeast and the research people placed in the Northeast. If the business is a Trading business, place the marketing and/or finance people in the Southeast. If the office is engaged in ʻentertainmentʼ, or houses a magazine business, then the important officers of the company should sit in the South(fame) or Southeast sectors.

The basis of these guidelines is the PaKua life situations method which identifies sectors with specific life situations. Use your own judgement when designing your office and allocating rooms for staff.

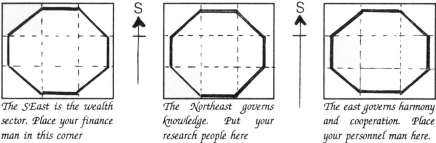

The SEast is the wealth sector. Place your finance man in this corner

The Northeast governs knowledge. Put your research people here

The east governs harmony and cooperation. Place your personnel man here.

In your office is located off a long corridor which open into other rooms, make certain they are brightly lit, and hang occasional windchimes to make the Chi settle. If you can help it avoid long narrow corridors. They are inauspicious for the occupants.

50. In recent years, due to increasing prosperity and growth in the size of many companies, PENTHOUSE office suites have become increasingly popular. These suites often house the chief executive and his personal staff, and are designed to include dining rooms, kitchens and even have luxurious trimmings like jacuzzis and indoor swimming pools. While all this glamour and luxury is impressive to bankers and potential joint venture partners, DO make sure feng shui features are taken into account, especially if large pools of water and indoor landscaping is involved. You must make sure the elements introduced are favourable to the chief executive and to the entrance door   to the penthouse. Otherwise, you could unknowingly be attracting shar Chi to your seat of power !

Most feng shui masters do not recommend having swimming pools at the top of buildings. This is aptly symbolised in the I Ching as "water above mountain", ie the trigram Kan which stands for water and also stands for danger, being placed above the trigram Ken, or mountain, represented by the tall building. The combination represents obstruction or unexpected danger to your business. It is also not conducive to negotiations for new undertakings or for partnerships requiring collaboration with other parties.

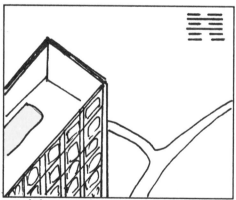

A pool of water at the top of a building is discouraged as it represents danger. Far better not to have it in your design

The author has seen at least three instances of extremely large corporations (in Malaysia) which collapsed barely three years after their respective bosses ignored feng shui advice, and incorporated luxurious indoor swimming pools into the penthouses of their corporate buildings. These had been located on the top floor of the building, representing grave danger to them.

51. When designing a GENERAL OFFICE, make sure furniture organization are symmetrical and balanced. Avoid arrangements that result in angles being formed, as in the case of L-shaped or U shaped desk arrangements or diagonally placed table groupings. Also try to avoid having staff sit directly facing each other in a confrontational mode.

Favourable desk and table arrangements affect office productivity by enhancing goodwill and cooperation amongst the staff.

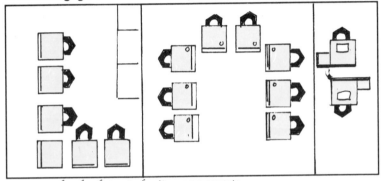

Some examples of unfortunate furniture arrangements

Offices with good feng shui rarely have problems of absenteeisms and constant ill health amongst employees. Lethargy, laziness and irresponsibility is also usually absent, or reduced if the feng shui of the office is made bright and energetic. If Chi is encouraged to flow through the office harmoniously, it will function like clockwork. Otherwise there can be constant problems, politickings and quarrels.

An L shaped arrangement cause frequent illnesses amongst staff, while a U shaped arrangement cause friction between employees. Desks placed face to face are deemed to be confrontational while diagonally arranged tables create disharmony and discord.
Classroom style arrangements are also not encouraged, as this too is deemed confrontational. The best arrangements are those which allow sufficient space for easy traffic movement in the office. Columns are incorporated into the design and camouflaged with plants. Mirrors are used to artificially enhance the feeling of space.

52. Finally a word about COLOUR schemes and colour combinations for the office. This is best worked out by using element analysis. The easy approach is to check your element based on your year of birth and design your colours accordingly. Do avoid elaborate wall designs which incorporate horizontal stripes; crosses; X's, and diamond shapes. If you use wall paper, select designs which harmonise with your element.

Let the colour scheme of the office blend into nuetral colours that do not pose a danger of clashing too badly with anyone's horoscope element. If you have taken the trouble to study what elements will bring you good fortune you can use this information to enhance the feng shui of your office by choosing colours that enhance your element.

Consider these rules:
* Wood is good fortune for Fire people. Use GREEN
* Fire is good for   Earth people. Use RED or shades of red.
* Earth is good for Metal people. Use BEIGE or BROWN.
* Metal is good for Water people. Use WHITE or GOLD.
* Water is good for Wood people. Use BLACK or shades of BLUE.
ON THE OTHER HAND:
* Wood destroys earth. So Earth people avoid GREEN.
* Earth destroys water. So water people avoid BEIGE or BROWN.
* Water destroys fire. So Fire people avoid BLACK or BLUE.
* Fire destroys metal. So metal people avoid RED.
* Metal destroys wood. So Wood people avoid GOLD OR WHITE.
AND AGAIN:
* Wood exhausts water. Water people avoid GREEN.
* Fire exhausts wood. Wood people avoid RED.
* Earth exhausts fire. Fire people avoid BEIGE or BROWN.
* Metal exhausts earth. Earth people avoid GOLD or WHITE.
* Water exhausts metal. Metal people avoid BLACK or BLUE.

Later, as your knowledge of feng shui increases you can use more advanced formulas to undertake element analysis with greater depth; and even introduce time and space dimensions to your feng shui calculations.

Chapter 4
FENG SHUI
of APARTMENTS & CONDOMINIUMS

53. Selecting a condominium or apartment which has good feng shui involves examining the surroundings of the apartment block itself, as well as studying the inside layout of the individual units. All guidelines given in earlier chapters pertaining to office buildings apply equally to residential apartment blocks. In assessing condominiums however, due importance must also be given to the residential aspects of the analyses ie bedrooms, dining rooms and kitchens. Features designed into condominiums and not for office buildings, eg. shape, size and location of swimming pools must also be considered.

One of the first things to look out for is the approach road leading to the apartment building. Driveways should be wide and curving rather than straight, and the size of the entrance must be balanced with the apartment block itself. Driveways should also be well lighted, and they should be of even width. If the apartment complex is made up of several interconnecetd buildings these should ideally have varying roof levels to resemble gently undulating hills. The apartment complex shown above has excellent landscape feng shui features. It obviously has been designed to attract auspicious Chi flow.

This apartment block has auspicious feng shui

54. Condominiums, like houses should not be located on hilltops where it is exposed to the winds, and where waters flow away rather than towards the building. This lack of protection creates a loss of the vital Chi, and good luck cannot be sustained. Incidentally, this same principle can also be applied to the building of "mansions in the sky", a recent phenomena on the Kuala Lumpur skyline.

Several new apartment blocks within Kuala Lumpur city have recently included impressive mansions, or penthouses with stately home facades, sitting above the multi storey apartment block. These penthouses look like huge mansions built at the very top of mountains. If the apartment block itself is also situated on elevated land, the feng shui of the whole block is considered inauspicious and is best avoided. If it is sited on level land, it is only the penthouse mansion which has unfortunate feng shui. The other units are not affected.

This is because, according to feng shui precepts, building one's home at the very top of mountains and hills is considered inauspicious.

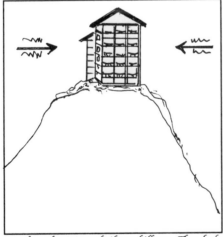

Avoid condominiums built on hilltops. They lack protection from winds, and water for prosperity.

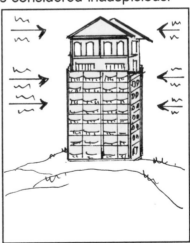

A "mansion in the sky" suffers from the same feng shui defect as one built on a hilltop.

93

55. All the guidelines regarding surrounding roads and rivers, as well as the direction and speed of traffic flow apply equally to apartment buildings as they do to office or commercial buildings, and in fact more so, because apartment blocks are residential places of abode. If Shar or poisonous Chi is hitting at the apartment building, residents will be unable to sleep restfully.

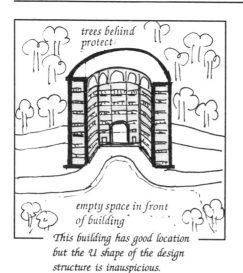

This building has good location but the U shape of the design structure is inauspicious.

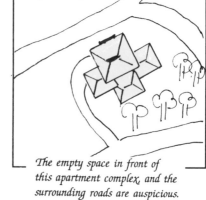

The empty space in front of this apartment complex, and the surrounding roads are auspicious.

When choosing a condominium to rent or buy, do not just look at existing roads. Analyse also the chances of there being any changes which are likely to be made to the road system around the building. Be especially wary about flyovers and elevated roads, (either existing or planned for the area) which curve too sharply around the building, as these represent knives, or bows with an arrow pointed at the building. With the city growing so fast, and with increasing traffic jams, new flyovers can very well be constructed at road junctions. So be careful.

Also be careful of surrounding roads that incline too sharply downhill towards the entrance of the apartment block as the Chi flow could be harmful. All slopes and banks should be gentle, not sharp nor too steep. The ideal configuration is for the apartment block to sit comfortably by the side of gently undulating land, and for roads to be "embracing" the building.

56. Apartment blocks located in good feng shui areas usually enjoy good landscape feng shui. Examples of good feng shui districts around Kuala Lumpur and Petaling Jaya are those areas which have prospered in the past ten years,·eg the Bangsar area, the]Damansara Areas in PJ and KL; the Ampang areas and so forth. However, it is vital to also realise that the landscapes in these areas have also been affected, sometimes adversley, by new developments - roads, flyovers, massive new buildings, signboards and other newly constructed structures.

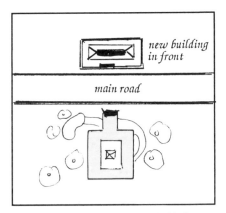

A taller building which directly blocks your main door can be harmful to you.

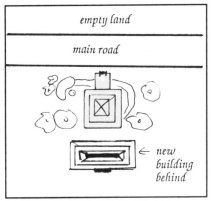

A taller building behind you is symbolically representative of the black turtle hill which protects.

In areas where special space has been set aside for gardens and playing fields, parks and open areas, it is good feng shui if the apartment building you are investigating directly faces such "breathing areas". In feng shui terms these are places where auspicious Chi accumulates to your advantage.

However, if the front of your building is inadvertently blocked by a massive new building which has been approved on the empty land in front, the feng shui is adversely affected. It is advisable not to buy or rent your new abode in the building which has been blocked. Where, on the other hand, the new building is located at the back of your apartment block, your feng shui has been enhanced because the new building then represents the black turtle which protects rather than harms.

57. The importance of investigating the prosperity of locations that interest you cannot be over stressed. Be alert to warning signs. Speak to shopkeepers in areas which have seen plenty of "new condomium activity". Then analyse the impact of these new developments on the apartment building that interests you.

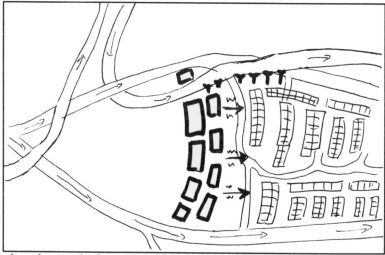

Shown here is a bustling section of PJ which had enjoyed much growth and prosperity until a gigantic flyover and eight massive new apartment blocks were built....

The prosperity of one of PJ's townships has been affected by the construction of eight massive apartment buildings, built side by side and forming a "wall" that completely blocks off Chi to the township, adversly affecting all houses with front doors facing the new buildings. More, a huge new flyover is being built at road junctions fringing the township. Houses whose front doors face the flyovers are also adversley affected. There has been an increase in the number of fatal accidents and burglaries in the area. In addition, retailers and shopkeepers have also reported that business which hitherto had been booming has also been on the wane.

Meanwhile, the apartment blocks themselves are not selling well as they collectively face a very big Y junction.

58. Apartment buildings should not be located on a ridge, since such locations are considered dangerous and inauspicious, there being totally no support for the residents. Similarly, having roads at both the front and back of a building that is located on a slope also results in bad feng shui for certain floors.

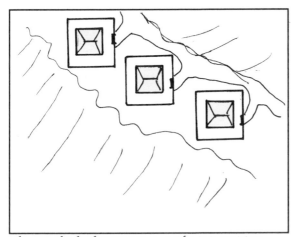
This row of 4 level apartments on a ridge is inauspicious

The feng shui of buildings or houses built on a hill ridge is dangerous, and is as bad as building on the tops of hills. There is a sorry lack of support for one's back. Such locations will suffer the bad CHi from winds; while not being able to tap into the good Chi of water, since the latter flow downhill and disappear.

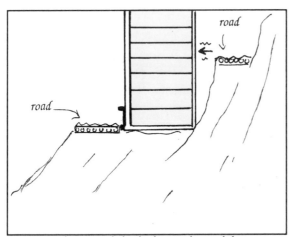
Apartment elevations of this kind are to be avoided

Another configuration that is best avoided is where there are roads at both the bottom and also halfway up the building. (see sketch). Residents will not enjoy good feng shui and those on floors "cut" by the top road will be especially unlucky since the road resembles a knife or blade cutting into the belly of the building. This "rule" also applies to bungalows and houses.

59. A SUMMARY OF GUIDELINES to look out for is useful when assessing an apartment block you are contemplating on buying or renting. Thus:

LOOK AT THE SURROUNDINGS:

* Avoid apartment buildings which appear "threatened" by massive or odd shaped structures nearby. These can be other buildings, big signboards, transmission towers, large water tanks, flyovers, or solid concrete walls and hills that directly front the building. These structures "block" Chi flow and spoil the natural harmony of these flows. It is advisable not to live facing these structures.

* Also avoid buildings whose entrance directly faces an oncoming straight road, or a Y junction. Straight, fast flowing rivers and straight railway tracks that appear to be pointed towards the entrance also bring bad luck to the building. If these roads and rivers are not "hitting" at the front entrance, the feng shui of the building is not affected. For this reason, developers who consult feng shui masters never locate entrances to their buildings facing a straight road. They are also careful about "poison arrows" and orientate the front entrance away from such arrows.

LOOK AT THE BUILDING ITSELF:

* There should be a main front entrance/door and a back door. Buildings without back doors are inauspicious.

* The driveway and approach road to the building should be of equal width. If it is gently curving or circular, it is auspicious.

* The building itself should have a regular shape, and if it comprise a cluster of buildings to form a complex, make sure the various structures balance and appear to be in harmony, ie the levels should appear to merge gently with each other.

* The building should also be in harmony with its surroundings, being neither too massive as the dwarf all others, or too small as to be dwarfes by surrounding buildings.

60. A view of WATER, artificial or natural often enhances the feng shui of any apartment building; but there are certain principles about water feng shui which are helpful to bear in mind.

Swimming pools are very popular features of condominium complexes, and generally, these bring auspicious feng shui to the residents. However, natural shaped pools (round, kidney or curved pools) are preferable to rectangular shaped pools, and where they have been landscaped the feng shui is more auspicious.

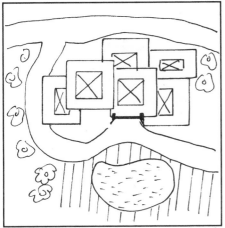

A kidney shaped pool which appears to hug the building is preferable to a rectangular pool

If the apartment building is built near mining pools or lakes, the feng shui is often regarded as auspicious. However, water should not be polluted or dirty. Nor should it be stagnant.

Waterfalls and fountains created as part of the landscape are also auspicious, especially where these face the main entrance of the building and can form part of the view for its residents.

Pools should not be located within the apartment block, either on the ground floor or on the top floor. Water, above or below, often spell danger and is never encouraged by feng shui masters. Pools should also be balanced in size, and should reflect the harmony of the elements. If your horoscope warns against the presence of the water element in your abode (eg if you are a fire element person) it is advisable to look for a condominium which does not have a swimming pool.

Another guideline is when the entrance of the building is facing the direction SOUTH which represents Fire, the pool should not be in front of the entrance since the water will destroy the fire element of the entrance. If the pool is in either the east, southeast, or north of the building, it is doubly auspicious since the presence of water in these locations will enhance the building's feng shui.

61. If there are RIVERS flowing past, or near to the condominium building, these should be slow-moving, clean and unpolluted. Fast flowing, straight rivers are purveyors of bad Chi and is inauspicious. Rivers which flow in front of buildings, especially if they are visible and are not blocked from view are auspicious.

The general guidelines on rivers and waterways given in an earlier chapter also apply to buildings. For individuals, it is always useful to check on their personal elements based on their year of birth. This will tell them if water is good for them.

In assessing the merits of a nearby river to the feng shui of a building, study the exact location of the building in relation to the river. First make certain no sharp edge of the river is "hitting" the building. Next examine whether the river is actually flowing past the entrance. This is the best way for the building to "tap" the lucky Chi flows of the river.

Residents will benefit in the form of money making opportunities, recognition, and success in various undertakings. Good water feng shui also brings prosperity and wealth in abundance.

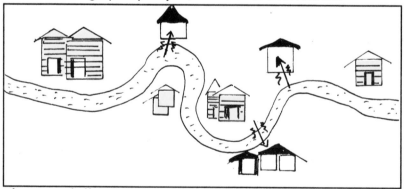

The auspicious buildings vis a vis this river are shaded. These are embraced by the river, and their front doors face the river.

If the river flows past the back entrance of the building, residents of the building can see opportunities but cannot benefit from these opportunities. Examples of good and bad orientations/locations along a river are shown in the sketch above.

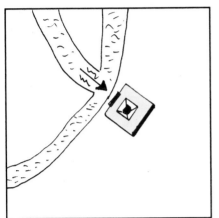

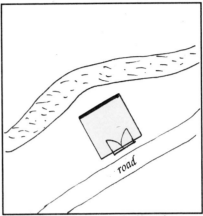

If the building faces a fork of a river, with a branch pointed at the entrance, it is inauspicious.

When a river flows past a building, but is not visible from the front door, there will be good opportunities, but these will be missed.

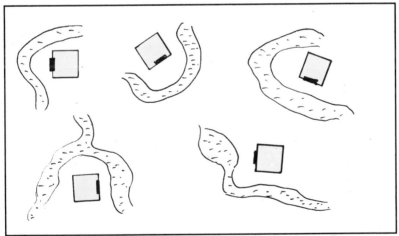

a series of auspicious placements of buildings based on the water dragon classic.

62. When viewing an apartment, examine layout plans carefully and get a feel for relative dimensions. First check the interior approach to the apartment. Ideally there should be a foyer that does not appear cramped. Lift and staircase areas should not be too narrow as Chi then tends to stagnate. Next examine the general layout plans to consider the feng shui aspects of how all the apartments are laid out vis-a-vis staircases and lifts.

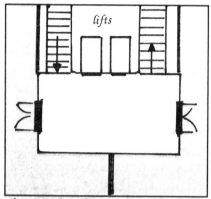

The approach to these two apartments is good. The stairs and lifts do not hurt the entrances.

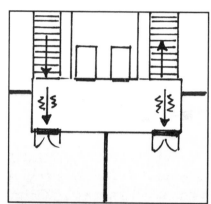

Staircase directly faces the entrance to the apartments. The feng shui is defective.

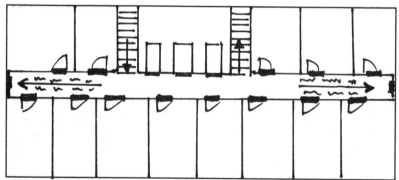

Apartments at the end of the corridor will suffer from Bad Chi flow, while the entrance doors to the other apartments do not align well with each other. The neighbours will quarrel.

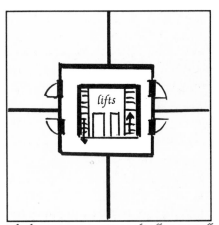
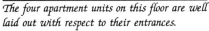

The four apartment units on this floor are well laid out with respect to their entrances.

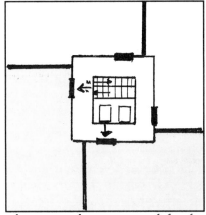

These entrance doorways to two of these four units (shaded) are hurt by the lift doors.

In the example below which shows an unlucky layout configuration all four doors actually form a straight line. These apartments are inauspicious and is best avoided. If you live in such an apartment, use a screen to block the back door and prevent Chi from flowing out too fast. The idea is to "break" the flow and force it to go round the screen. This enables auspicious Chi to settle and accumulate within the apartment, thereby bringing good luck.

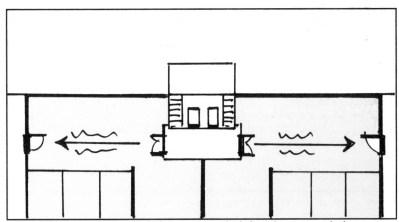

The entrances to these units and their respective back doors form a straight line. BAD !

63. When selecting an apartment choose one whose front door faces your best DIRECTION, paying careful attention that the door is not at the same time "hurt" by other doors or staircases etc. For families, the door should generally be auspicious for the head of the household, or the breadwinner of the family. To check your directions use the tables at the back of the book.

Do remember that directions are taken from INSIDE THE APARTMENT looking out. Use a good prismatic compass so that you are as accurate as possible. If you find it difficult to decide whether the front door should face your direction or that of your husband's direction, balance the favourable features between each other by checking the directions of other important locations, ie the main bedroom, the kitchen stove or secondary doors. Secondary doors (opening to balconies or garden patios) often supplement the main door in as far as admitting Chi into the household is concerned. Where the direction of secondary doors are also auspicious, keep them opened!

This occurs when both doors are facing directions that complement each other. Thus EAST group directions are north, south, east and southeast. WEST group directions are west, northwest, southwest and northeast. Directions belonging to the same group complement and reinforce each other. Do check if you are an East or a West person.

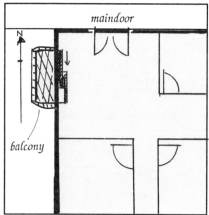

The main door faces north. The secondary door faces west. They are incompatible.

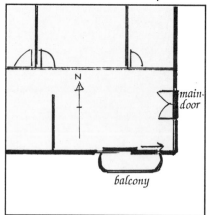

The main door faces east and the balcony door faces south. Both directions belong to the East group. The doors reinforce each other.

64. Upon entering the apartment, or the inside of a house, the immediate area near the door should not be narrow and cramped. Ideally upon opening the main door you should have good size view of the living room. The diagonal corner furthest away from the main door is an auspicious corner. Make sure there is no protruding column in this corner.

 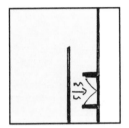 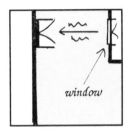

window

The three sketches above show inauspicious foyer areas. The first faces a toilet; the second is narrow and cramped and the third faces a window. All three are examples of inauspicious feng shui, and is best avoided. If you are already staying in such an apartment, use wall mirrors to visually enlarge the area and keep the window closed. In the case of a toilet, the best thing to do is not to use it at all, or change its entrance. As a general rule toilets should never face important doors, or doors to important rooms.

In the diagram on the right, the most auspicious corner within view of the front door is indicated with an arrow. Here the corner is flawed by a protruding column. Use plants to nullify the effect of this column. If there is no column, you can enhance feng shui by placing an aquarium here ie if your horoscope is compatible. Check this by making sure your year element is not Fire, because fire is destroyed by water. Plants are good for fire people.

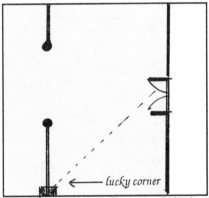

← lucky corner

The luckiest corner within view of the front door is shown here. Landsacpe this corner.

65. In apartment living, balconies which face beautiful views are highly prized. However do make certain that there are not too many balconies in an apartment, or worse, that two balconies are directly opposite each other. This causes Chi to flow in and out too easily and is inauspicious.

The most obvious example of offending balconies (no matter how beautiful the views) are when the balcony attached to the living room directly faces the balcony attached to the dining room. This is indicated in the sketch on this page. Where there are balconies in different rooms the feng shui is not adversly affected, eg in the case of there being balconies for all the bedrooms. This is because the Chi flow has had a chance to flow nicely through the apartment.

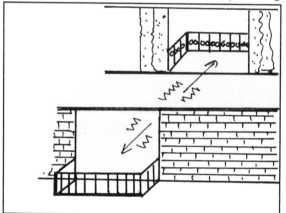

Balconies directly facing each other cause Chi to flow out even as it enters. This has an adverse effect on the feng shui of the apartment.

In addition, it is useful to also ensure that the design of the grills on the balconies (and for the windows) are not shaped as sharp arrows pointed inwards. Always remember that anything angled, pointed and sharp facing you, your main door, or your apartment is inauspicious, and such views should be screened off. It is best to be on the lookout for these objects and structures while you are still house hunting. The effect of some pointed "arrows" can be dissipated with feng shui antidotes. But not all. Thus it is better not to have them within sight at all !

Like balconies, there should also not be too many windows or have the windows facing each other in a way which encourages Chi to flow in and out of the apartment too rapidly. The ratio of windows to doors in an apartment should not exceed three to one.

66. Be wary of decorative PILLARS inside an apartment. Round pillars are preferable to square pillars, and they should not overwhelm the room. Do not have decorative pillars unless your apartment is sufficiently high and spacious. Stand alone pillars should not face doors or block seating arrangements.

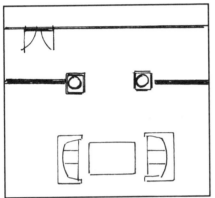

These round pillars frame the entranceway to the living room and do not harm the front door.

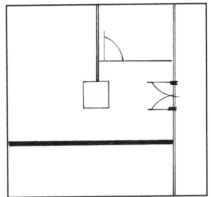

This square pillar is facing the front door. An example of very bad feng shui

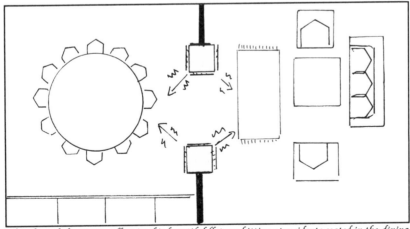

The edges of the square pillars in this beautiful flat are hitting at residents seated in the dining and living areas, but because they have been "wrapped" with mirrors, they are acceptable.

67. The interior LAYOUT of apartments should be conducive to the smooth flow and accumulation of good luck Chi. Thus the flow of movement and traffic inside should meander and circulate rather than gushing in a straight line. Long narrow corridors are discouraged, as are too many doors/windows facing each other in a straight line. Dark, cramped corners should be brightly lighted, and room dimensions should balance.

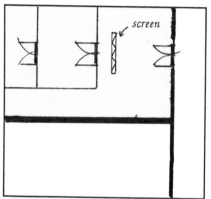

Three doors in a row within an apartment should be corrected, either with a screen or by hanging windchimes on the middle door.

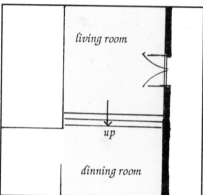

Where there are split levels, the higher level should be the dining room. The living room should be located on the lower level.

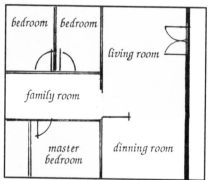

Living rooms (yang) must be larger than every bedroom (yin). The male yang must be stronger than the female yin for there to be harmony.

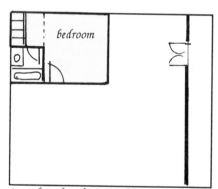

Irregular shaped rooms like the L shaped bedroom here are inauspicious. try to camouflage it with cupboards or a curtain.

68. The placement of rooms and as well as the furniture within often affects resident's behaviour. LIVING ROOMS should ideally be near the main entrance to symbolise the "home, welcoming residents" each day. The arrangement of furniture should harmonise. Avoid asymmetrical or L shaped arrangements.

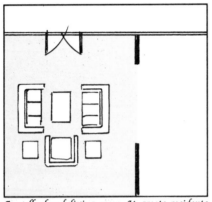

A well placed living room. It greets residents and guests with a welcoming ambience, and the furniture arrangement is balanced. GOOD.

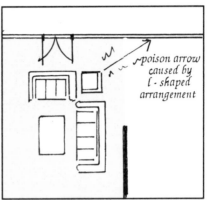

An awkwardly placed living room. The arrangement of furniture also creates a poison arrow aimed at the adjoining room. BAD.

Living rooms with a pleasant view, eg water, blue skies or beautiful scenery brings good luck and good feelings to the household.

Views of poison arrows or walls of other buildings should be curtained off to shut out the bad Chi emanating from these structures.

69. If you have a STUDY in your apartment, placing it near the front door encourages work, reading and studying. This is regarded as auspicious for working people or households with school going children. Pay special attention however to the arrangement of furniture inside studies.

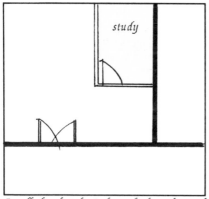

A well placed study. It faces the front door and encourages residents to work and/or study. Do ensure its door does not face a toilet.

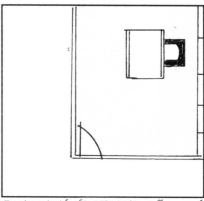

Furniture inside this STUDY is well arranged. The desk is in the far diagonal corner facing the door. This is an auspicious placement.

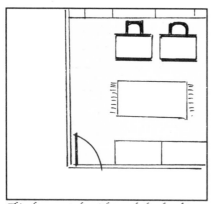

This shows a study with two desks placed in an auspicious arrangement. Suitable for households with two school age children.

Good arrangement of desk, but exposed book shelves are inauspicious. They symbolise blades cutting at occupants. Close them with doors.

70. Careful attention must be paid to the location of KITCHENS and the placement of STOVES. Besides affecting residents luck, this room is the source of food, and inauspicious orientations will create problems for residents.

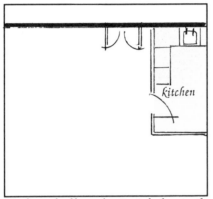

Kitchens should not be situated close to the main door. Unfavourable for children who will grow fat, and tend to ignore their studies !

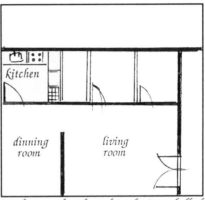

Kitchens are best located in the inner half of an apartment, out of view of the front door.

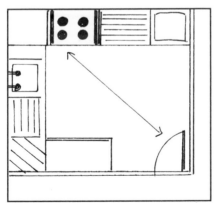

Kitchen layouts should have the stoves (cooking area) placed diagonally opposite the door.

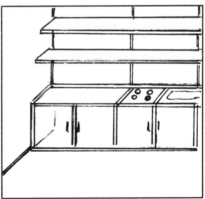

Built-in shelves in a kitchen should be closed with doors. Exposed shelves act like cutting blades which hurt occupants.

71. The BATHROOM or TOILET placement in an apartment is important because these rooms tend to exert inauspicious influences if located in the wrong places. Thus entrances to toilets should never be placed within sight of the front door.

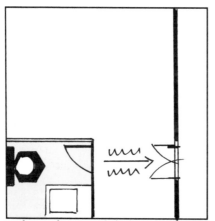

Toilets within view of the front door cause ill health and loss of wealth. The symbolism is that money entering the home gets flushed away.

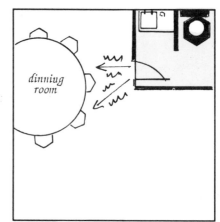

Toilets should also not be within view of dining rooms and living rooms. Keep doors closed or build a small wall divider inside bathrooms.

Under the PaKua LoShu system of Feng Shui which calculates auspicious and inauspicious locations based on one's natal chart, toilets and bathrooms are supposed to be placed in the identified "inauspicious" or unlucky sectors, so that the toilet "presses against their bad luck". The location varies between individuals.

Readers may investigate their relevant lucky and unlucky sectors according to their date of birth, (based on this system) in Chapter Nine which summarises some of the more practical formulas of Feng Shui. Those who wish to have a more comprehensive explanation of the PaKua LoShu formula and its usage are referred to the author's book on this subject entitled APPLIED FENG SHUI.

All other rooms and their locations can also be similarly analysed based on this PaKua LoShu formula. The rule is that bedrooms, studies, living rooms and dining rooms should be in auspicious locations while toilets and kitchens should be in unlucky locations.

72. Placement of BEDROOMS affect the feng shui of residents as this is where they rest and regain energy lost during the day. While there are formulas which pinpoint specific auspicious locations, certain guidelines should also be observed eg. doors to bedrooms should not be within sight of the front door. Inside bedrooms, beds should not be placed with the head under an overhead beam, or with the door behind the bed ...

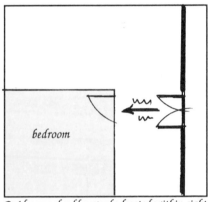

Be4drooms should never be located within sight of the front door. This depletes energy from residents, who will thus be tired & listless.

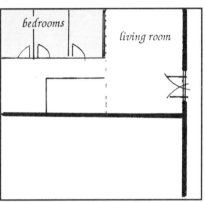

Bedrooms are best located deep inside the apartment. Every bedroom should also be smaller than the living room.

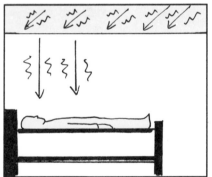

Beds should never be placed beneath an overhead beam. This cause illness, bad luck and headaches. Rearrange the bed !

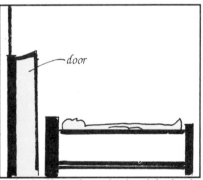

Beds should not have the door behind. This causes instability of fortunes.

MIRRORS: BAD IN THE BEDROOM

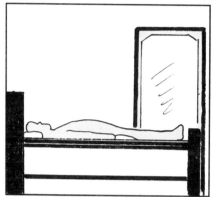

Having a mirror at the foot of the bed is bad luck. Occupant of bed could be frightened by his own reflection. It is also bad feng shui.

Do be careful when placing mirrors in the bedroom. Most feng shui Masters discourage having mirrors in the bedroom at all, and in fact encourage vanity and dressing tables to be placed in a separate area. The guideline here is to make sure the mirror is not refelcting the bed. If it is facing the same direction as the bed it will not do any harm. Otherwise, mirrors in the bedroom cause strife and discord between husband and wife and between siblings sharing the bedroom.

MIRRORS: GOOD IN THE DINING AREA

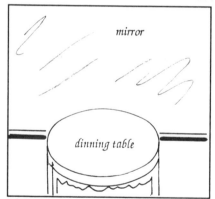

Mirrors in the dining room bring wealth and an increase in income levels to the household.

Feng Shui Masters from Hong Kong are very keen on having wall mirrors in the dining room. They believe that this symbolises a doubling of food on the table, and also reflects abundance and plenty. If you plan to adopt this recommendation, do make sure the mirror covers the wall in a way which does not cut off the residents feet or head. This means the mirror should be sufficiently large. Do NOT use mirror tiles. If you cannot afford a one piece wall mirror that is large enough to cover the whole wall, do not compromise by using the cheaper wall tiles. These have the effect of "cutting" at residents and is definately inauspicious. Also make sure the mirror is not reflecting anything sharp or pointed which you may have inadavertently placed in the dining room area. Finally, if there is a toilet adjoining the dining room, a mirror might be reflecting it. If so, it is better not to have the mirror at all.

SAMPLE LAYOUT OF APARTMENT

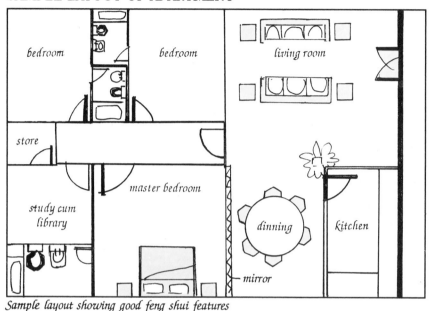

Sample layout showing good feng shui features

In the example note the following good feng shui features:
* The main door opens to the living room.
  It is unencumbered by either a toilet, a wall or cramped space.
* The public areas (dining & living rooms) are in the outer half of the apartment while the bedrooms are located in the inner half.
* The kitchen is located next to the dining area which is good.
* The dining room wall is mirrored, thereby doubling food on the table - an auspicious indication.
* There are no protruding corners in this apartment.

* The master bedroom is in its best location vis-a-vis the main door.
* There are no pillars or columns to disturb the flow of good Chi.
* The doors and entrances have been designed to let the Chi meander through the apartment, thus allowing it to accumulate.
* The size of the rooms are balanced.
  Not too big in relation to each other, nor too small.
* The living room is larger than the bedrooms. Yang dominates, and is therefore auspicious for the family breadwinner.

73. There are several important pointers and tips about internal layout of rooms which are useful to bear in mind when shopping for an apartment. These are summarised here for easy reference.

* All apartments can be symbolically divided into inner and outer halves. Bedrooms and kitchens should always be in the inner half while living and dining areas in the outer half.

* Kitchens should never be placed in the centre of homes as this cause illness. Bathrooms too should never be in the centre of the house as this cause money to drain away. Bathrooms should also not be directly facing the kitchen - as this cause finances and health to suffer. Since the kitchen symbolise food, this also cause it to be "flushed away" thereby symbolising loss.

* The master bedroom is regarded as one of the most important rooms in the house. If it can be located in the opposite corner of the apartment from the main door, the location is auspicious since it allows residents to have maximum control over their fortunes and destinies, and is also conducive to good luck.

* Meanwhile, the bedroom door should not face another door which leads to the bathroom. Attached bathrooms are acceptable if the door to the bathroom does not face the entrance door to the bedroom.

* All bedrooms should be far away from the front door to enjoy peace and harmony. For double storey houses this is rarely a problem since bedrooms are usually located upstairs, but in apartments, special care must be devoted to ensuring that none of the bedrooms are within view of the main front door of the apartment.

* None of the rooms should sit at the end of a long corridor as this causes illness and bad luck to the occupant.

* If possible let the centre of the apartment be an area for all members of the family - ie a family room. This is because the centre symbolises the centre of the pa kua, and represents the essence of the household. Definately no bathrooms in the centre.

PART TWO
PRACTICAL WAYS TO IMPROVE FENG SHUI

Chapter 5
FENG SHUI ENHANCING TECHNIQUES

74. It is definately possible to improve the feng shui of houses and apartments; offices and business premises. The suggested methods can be broadly divided into two categories ie the method using feng shui enhancing tools and the method using ancient classical formulas. In this chapter and the next, the methods covered fall into the first category.

Not everyone is fortunate enough to be able to design and build their homes and offices, and are thus unable to factor in all the features necessary to enjoy good feng shui. It is also rare for anyone to find a ready made good feng shui house or office.

However, since feng shui is a dynamic science based on principles of balance, harmony, symbolism and the effective harnessing of good Chi flows, existing layouts and structures can be "corrected" or modified to improve feng shui.

The first step in enhancing feng shui is to understand the underlying basic principles behind the practice, and to adopt a systematic approach when investigating surrounding landscapes and assessing structures. Start by taking the defensive approach. Protect your homes and offices from killing shar Chi that are created by the presence of malignant poison arrows which point at your place of abode or your place of work.

These poison arrows are symbolic instruments or structures which are pointed, straight, angled, sharp or hostile. They are dangerous when directly aimed at your main door or entrance. Once you have identified potentially damaging arrows near or around you, the next step is to diffuse or deflect the killing effect of these arrows.

This is done by either blocking off a view of these arrows, or by using something to "counter" its effect. Or you can also deflect its vibrations by re-orientating your door such that it escapes the impact of the arrow. Remember that poison Chi which brings bad luck travels in a straight line. Understanding this enables you to be very creative in your efforts to "block" or "ward off" the effect of poison arrows.

75. There are several very effective defensive measures you can use to escape the effect of poison arrows. The idea is to effectively block off a view of the offending structure, or to diffuse the flow of poison Chi aimed at your door.

DEFLECTING POISON ARROWS
* USE TREES TO BLOCK OFF VIEW
* USE CANNONS TO COUNTER POWERFUL ARROW
* CHANGE DIRECTION/PLACEMENT OF DOOR
* BUILD A WALL TO DEMARCATE
* USE PAKUA MIRROR TO REFLECT BACK

USING TREES

Probably the most effective and easiest method to shield your house from poison arrows caused by an angled roof line, or by a church spire, or offending flyovers, or a straight road facing your house, or other equally dangerous structures, is to grow a clump of trees in a way which completely blocks off a view of the offending structure(s). You must grow a few trees, not just one tree because a single tree can cause more harm than good. The trees chosen should have broad leaves. Trees with pointed leaves are not auspicious.

Trees take time to grow, and while waiting it may be useful to use a PaKua mirror to deflect the poison Chi first.

Sometimes, because the Chi coming from the structure is too powerful, either your PaKua may fall off or the trees may die. In such cases, stronger measures may be called for.

TREES shielding a house from CROSSROADS

TREES shielding a house from an angled roofline from the house opposite

USING CANNONS

This is a very powerful method of deflecting the damaging Chi flows caused by massive poison arrows. Cannons represent hostile killing machines and should not be used except as a last resort. The countering vibrations which the presence of a cannon creates is sometimes so powerful that residents can become too aggressive. So do use cannons with great care and caution. They will not merely "deflect" the poison arrow; cannons actually destroy the feng shui of the area or house or building at which it is pointed. And usually, the larger and older the cannon, the more powerful will be the effect. In your attempt to improve your own feng shui, you must guard against the temptation of destroying your neighbour's feng shui. Do remember that there is a retaliation possibility. Use discretion.

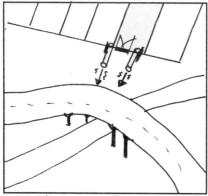

A pair of cannons aimed at deadly shar Chi created by the flyover in front of the house

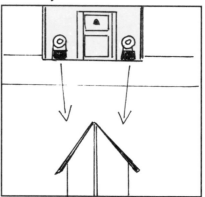

Cannons aimed at angled roofline from the house opposite can be too damaging. Be careful.

In Malaysia, a good place to look for miniature cannons is Sarawak. These are better to use than large antique cannons as they are not as "fierce" in their effect. It is also interesting to note that there are male (yang) cannons and female (yin) cannons. It is believed that cannons should be used as a pair to reduce their fierce effect. When positioned as a single cannon, the female is more powerful than the male.

In Kuala Lumpur, along Jalan Raja Chulan, a cannon was installed outside a building to protect it from the bad effects of a huge X shaped pair of elevators from the building across the road. Since installing the cannon, business improved, but for the occupants of the building across the road the story has not been so good !

CHANGING THE DIRECTION OF YOUR DOOR

Another approach to cope with poison arrows, is to re-orientate your front door such that it does not directly face the offending presence. this is an excellent way of deflecting problems caused by straight roads at a T junction, or a massive structure in front of your house, like a newly built multi storey apartment block. When using this approach, it is perhaps useful to countercheck your auspicious direction. Do this by referring to the relevant formula given under PaKua LoShu feng shui in Chapter Nine.

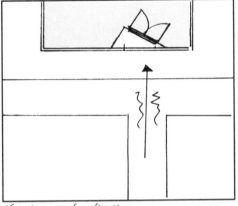

Changing your door direction is an excellent way of countering poison arrows.

In the example shown on the left, the change in door direction completely re-orientates the feng shui of this house. Do note that while doing this will deflect shar Chi caused by the offending road, it also has other effects under compass feng shui formulas, and it is usefult to check these out before going to the trouble of changing direction.

Main door directions are extremely important in the context of feng shui practice. Different texts offer different advice on this matter, as do the different schools of feng shui. eg the Yang Dwelling Classic advices facing south; while advocating avoiding Southeast and North. The PaKua LoShu method advise orienting the door according to one's auspicious directions. At the same time, another school of feng shui which introduces a time element to the practise advise orienting the main door according to calculations based on the "Moving star" method. This latter method is based on the 20 year cycle of auspicious and inauspicious directions.

For the beginner, it is sufficient that you avoid the poison arrows, and deflect its killing Chi from hitting your door. For a more advanced approach towards the siting of main doors learn the formulas in Chapter Nine thoroughly before attempting them.

BUILDING A WALL TO DEMARCATE

Yet another effective method of combating the bad forces of "killing Chi" caused by poison arrows, is to build a wall that clearly demarcates your compound, while at the same time effectively blocking out a view of the offending arrow or structure. This is illustrated in the diagram below. Here two offending roads pointed straight at the front door is effectively "shut out" by the solid brick wall. These walls should be at least five feet high to be effective.

The clump of trees at the back of the house provides symbolic protection to the household while the arrangement of the driveway ensures that the flow of Chi into the home is smooth and harmonious.

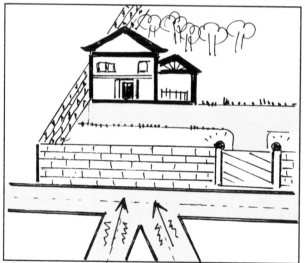

The construction of a wall effectively shuts out the bad forces caused by the two straight roads pointed at the front door.

There are several other ways of using a solid brick wall to fend off bad or undesirable feng shui. Apart from other structures which can overwhelm the Chi of your house, walls are also effective in cutting off the bad effect of a public drain that is polluted or dirty; or a drain that is flowing in a wrong direction ie a direction that is "bad" for you. Generally waterways, including drains should flow from east to west, ie from the higher elevated dragon side to the lower tiger side. If the drain flows in the wrong, ie opposite direction, no need to fret - merely build a wall to block off its influence on your land. This was exactly the problem faced by a professional woman whose career was getting nowhere. Immediately after her wall was built she went from one meaningful promotion to another !

76. While using protective measures to diffuse the influence of killing Chi from outside structures and features, it is also necessary to systematically identify the features within the interiors of a house, office or shop, and then to diffuse their inauspicious effects. In this way, feng shui problems caused by overhead beams, protruding corners, slanted or unproportional sized doors, square columns and irregular shaped rooms can be "corrected" by installing simple feng shui cures or antidotes. Examples of these cures are illustrated in the diagrams below.

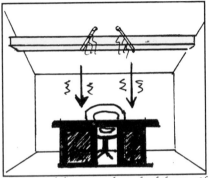

Never sit below exposed overhead beams. If these beams "threaten" dining or work tables hang two flutes tied with red thread.

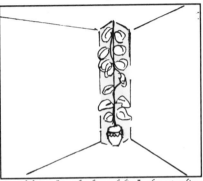

Avoid being "in the line of fire" of protruding corners. If one is hitting at a favourite chair, use a creeper plant to diffuse the sharp corner.

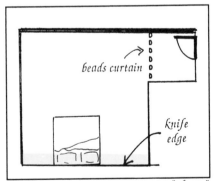

An L shaped bedroom can represent a "cleaver" and putting the bed on the "knife edge" is dangerous. Use beaded curtains as shown.

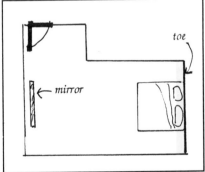

An L shaped room can also resemble a "boot". If the bed is located in the toe it is bad. Use a mirror to "reflect" the bed to the other side.

77. All DOORS and entrances within a house or apartment can be enhanced with a little bit of ingenuity and some knowledge of the feng shui meanings of the eight compass directions and orientations. There are special techniques based on specific feng shui formulas, and there are also general guidelines that can be utilised to intensify your sense of well being and promote good healthy Chi flows that amplify good feng shui.

The entrance to a room sets the "tone" of the house or office. Once you become aware of this, you will begin to notice that certain houses and rooms are more welcoming than others, some give you a happy comfortable sense of well being, others put you off immediately. This is the result of favourable or unfavourable Chi flows caused by the location, shape, size and orientation of doors. The ideal is to enter a wide, well lighted room or foyer. Doors should open to the broadest part of a room, and have maximum view of the interior. The lobby area should not be narrow and cramped. This causes residents' luck to dry up, causes illness and chokes the flow of Chi. A mirror corrects this particular feng shui malaise, but an appealing painting and a bright overhead light will also do the trick ! Bright lights expand Chi and encourages it to circulate benevolently upwards.

Never allow strong drafts of air to enter the front door - its invisible force will cause money and luck to drain out of the house. Use a screen, if necessary to "slow down" air flows

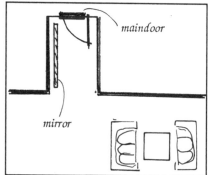

A narrow lobby area at the entrance stifles feng shui, causing ill health and creating bad luck. Use a mirror to "expand" the area.

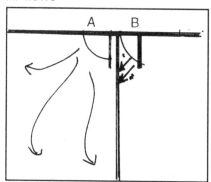

Doors should open to the widest area of the room (shown in A), and not open to a wall (as shown in B). Change hinges of B type doors. to A ty

78. DOORS within a home can be used to strongly enhance certain aspects of your feng shui. Here is a method that is worth considering and implementing. It draws on the PaKua's eight directions, and applying the symbolic meanings of each of these compass directions. You can use the method to enhance front doors or secondary doors within a house/apartment.

The direction a door faces can, to some extent, determine your destiny. A unique system used quite extensively in Hong Kong attaches special meanings to the eight compass directions. Thus doors facing each of these directions, especially when frequently used by residents and "activated" by hanging suitable feng shui "tools" will bestow different types of good fortune.

THUS:
* A door facing NORTH brings great business success. North is also Water. Enhance the door further by hanging a windchime (metal) which produces water in the cycle of elements. Alternately, locate a small fish pond or an aquarium near the door. This magnifies the symbolism further.
* A door facing SOUTH bestows fame for the person using this door frequently eg if the door to your study faces south, (looking from inside the room) you will become well known. If you wish to augment this further, hang a very bright light above the door, inside or outside, to magnify the element of fire. Or place a plant (wood) near the door to "feed the fire".
* A door facing EAST enhances family togetherness. East is wood, and to enhance this door, "use water to produce wood". And keep a plant nearby. This door will be ideal as the entrance to the family room.
* A door facing WEST intensifies the good fortune of the children of the household. Because west is metal, you can enhance this door by hanging a windchime or placing a rock crystal on display near the door. Doors to your children's bedrooms should ideally face west to tap this good fortune.
* A door facing NORTHEAST (earth) magnifies scholarly success and intelligence. It is also excellent for children's rooms. Intensify the door's effect by hanging a very bright light near it. (Fire produces earth)
* A door facing NORTHWEST (metal) enhances travel and overseas contacts. Enhance it with a windchime, or with plants.
* A door facing SOUTHEAST brings wealth and prosperity. Enhance this wood element door by having plants and an aquarium nearby.
* A door facing SOUTHWEST (earth) brings you a good spouse and an excellent marriage. Enhance this door with a bright red light !

DOOR ALIGNMENTS

are vital to promoting harmony within the home. They should face each other directly and not overlap. There is one taboo however: two bathroom doors should not face each other.

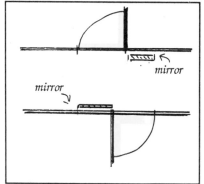

Parallel doors facing each other should be directly aligned to each other. Otherwise, use a mirror as shown in the sketch above.

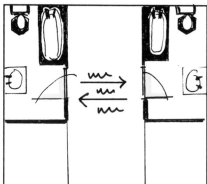

Two bathroom doors should not face each other directly. This is one of the crucial taboos of feng shui guidelines.

DOOR SIZE

should be equal, if the doors are facing opposite each other. Unequal size doors are potentially harmful to the occupant of the room with the smaller door, unless it opens to a room smaller than the other room.

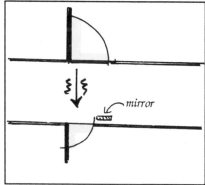

Different size doors facing each other is potentially harmful to the resident of the room with the smaller door. Use a mirror to correct.

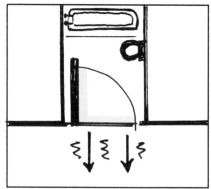

A large or oversize door leading into a small bathroom cause health problems. Hang a crystal outside the door to correct the imbalance.

SLANTED DOORS

are extremely dangerous. Try to avoid having them completely. Such doors exist in houses or apartments with slanted ceilings, and they have the potential to destroy the feng shui of the entire apartment because they symbolise a sharp knife or blade inside the belly of the home. The bad feng shui manifests itself in unexpected tragic consequences like death or severe illness to a member of the household.

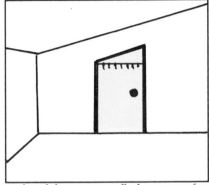

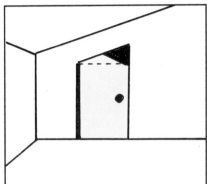

A slanted door is potentially disastrous to feng shui. Hang a red tasselled curtain to divide the door into two parts to correct the situation.

Another cure for a slanted door is to paint the top part of a complemetary slant thereby creating a symmetrical shape to the door.

As a general rule there should not be too many doors along the same axis of a house. Nor should three or more doors be arranged in a straight line. This is a dangerous alignment. Place a screen between the doors if your home has such a feature since the flow of Chi is too strong and must be slowed down.

If there are unused or "dead" doors in the home, this can cause severe misunderstandings between parents and children, and between siblings. Examples of such un-used doors include doors to store rooms, as well as doors to rooms of children who are studying abroad. An effective antidote to their ill effects is to install a mirror outside the door. This has the effect of making the offending door "disappear". Unless you do something about such un-used doors, the bad feng shui can affect the luck of your children overseas, even though they may not be living at home.

79. One important feature to bear in mind when attempting to enhance your feng shui is the need to ACHIEVE YIN/YANG BALANCE as much as you can, both inside and outside your home, apartment or office. This is best done by thoroughly familiarising yourself with the symbols of YIN and the symbols of YANG, and then understanding what is meant by balance.

A harmonious balance of Chi brings great prosperity, and this balance is achieved in specific ways. According to feng shui, balance refers to a balance of the YIN and the YANG forces, and to achieve this balance, one must know what constitues YIN and what constitutes YANG. As well as their characteristics.

The YIN YANG symbol

Thus light and darkness, distance and nearness, solid and space, light and heavy, must complement to create a balanced base from which the residents Chi can create a vital life force and bring prosperity. How is this done ?   How is balance achieved ?

By ensuring there is not too much YIN and not too much YANG !

YIN is dark, the Earth, heavy, cold, turgid. It is Water, the moon; it is queit, and it is the silence of tombs. In terms of the elements, Metal is lesser Yin and Water is greater Yin.

YANG is light, Heaven, clarity, fire, the sun and life in all its manifestations. It is noise, warmth and bright sunshine. In terms of the elements, Wood is lesser Yang and Fire is greater Yang.

When arranging your furniture, air conditioning your rooms, choosing your colour schemes, designing your layout plans, and purchasing your display items keep the Yin Yang balance in mind.
Make sure the house is not too bright everywhere, in every corner. Vary with shaded areas. Likewise let not every room be noisy and loud. Have rooms for rest and relaxation (which should be queit) and rooms for music and entertainment (noise). Stay balanced !

80. A very novel method of enhancing feng shui recommended by certain masters is the use of the "channelling method". This method uses long, hollow bamboo or copper rods that are embedded upright, into the ground. It is believed that this method allows the practitioner to directly tap into the EARTH'S CHI. If effectively done, it is claimed that this method will create prosperity and abundant good luck for residents.

This is a very popular method with the Hokkien dialect group, and is practised more in Taiwan than in Hong Kong. The method entails "fixing" a hollow rod into the earth as this is believed to channel, ie bring up, the earth's Chi which is all powerful !

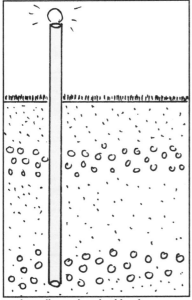

A channelling rod made of bamboo or copper effectively brings up the Earth's Chi, which in turn brings prosperity.

Some practitioners also attach a bright light at the top of the rod which is above ground, to further encourage the Chi to rise.

If you wish to try this method it is advisable to do it in the "Earth sectors" of your compound ie either the Southwest sector or the North East sector. These sectors represent the marriage and the scholarly success sectors respectively.

You may also use this method in the Metal sectors since Earth produces Metal (see next page). The Metal Sectors are the West (representing fame for the children) and Northwest (representing success in travel and overseas contacts).

Practitioners of the channelling method claim that the auspicious results of this method can be felt almost immediately, especially in terms of benefits to children. The width of the rods can be variable. But be careful that the hollow rod does not get   blocked.

81. Enhancing feng shui also requires clever usage of element relationships. When we refer to the ELEMENTS - water, wood, fire, earth and metal - it is important to recognise that there are two basic rules to follow; one, their productive and destructive relationship must be thoroughly understood; and two, they must be applied symbolically. We refer not to substance and matter, but to process and correlations.

The Five Elements and their relationships is a vital component of feng shui practice. Use the various representations summarised here to improve your application of the various techniques and methods offered in this book. Bear in mind that feng shui practice is based on the PaKua symbol which is made up of eight sides; each, representing a compass direction as well as a TRIGRAM that is arranged according to the Later Heaven Sequence, and this marries an element to each of the directions. As shown in the diagram below.

You can enhance the element represented by any direction, by simply using the various symbols represented by each element. Thus if you wish to enhance the metal element, you may display a lion or a windchime or a golden rooster in the corner corresponding to that element !

And if you wish to enhance the wood element, you can use the colour green, or you can use plants or display a porcelain tiger or rabbit in the relevant corner.

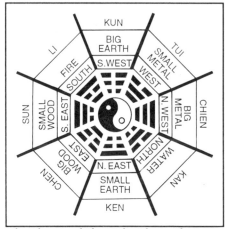

The Elements of the Eight sides in the PaKua Symbol based on the later heaven Arrangement

When using elements to enhance feng shui, it is necessary to check the productive and destructive cycles of the elements. It is important not to make the mistake of activating the wrong element. This is the reason why feng shui masters warn against placing aquariums and windchimes etc in just any corner of the home.

THE ELEMENT RELATIONSHIPS REPEATED:

FIRE produces EARTH which produces METAL which produces WATER which produces WOOD which produces FIRE.

and therefore ...
FIRE exhausts WOOD which exhausts WATER which exhausts METAL which exhausts EARTH which exhausts FIRE.

meanwhile ...
FIRE destroys METAL which destroys WOOD which destroys EARTH which destroys WATER which destroys FIRE.

however ...
SMALL METAL produces WOOD (Knife carves out furniture)
SMALL FIRE produces METAL (Heat produces gold ornaments)

Having understood the relationships between the elements, study the symbols attached to each of these elements. Using these symbols you are now in a position to "activate" any element belonging to each of the directions, thereby enhancing a door, a bed, a stove, a special room or even a specific member of the household.

WOOD: Springtime, eldest son or daughter, plants, trees, the colour green, the Tiger, and the Rabbit. South East & East.

FIRE: Summertime, middle-aged woman, lights, the sun, the colour red, the Snake, and the Horse. South.

EARTH: Crystal, boulders, stones, the colour yellow, the Ox, the Dragon, the Goat/sheep, and the Dog. Centre, South West & North East.

METAL: Autumn, young girl, old man, mouth, the colour white or gold, windchimes, coins, the Lion, the Monkey and the Rooster. West and North West.

WATER: Winter, middleaged man, waterfall, fountain, acquarium, the colours blue and black, the Rat and the Pig. North.

Chapter 6
FENG SHUI ENHANCING TOOLS

82. Of the various feng shui enhancing tools, probably the most widely used by Masters is the MIRROR, which, besides being excellent for interior design, are also effective for a variety of feng shui uses. Mirrors draw in "lucky" views of rivers, lakes and mountains, as well as other positive forces. They reflect light and food on the table thereby "doubling" the effect of abundance. Used on doors and narrow corners, they "expand" the feeling of space thereby attracting and trapping good Chi flows.

The effect of mirrors is mainly visual, to create healthy optic depth and distance to small rooms and unused doors. Irregular shaped rooms that are deemed incomplete can be corrected by installing wall mirrors which have the effect of "extending" the space beyond the wall. Cramped entrance halls can also be similarly extended, although some feng shui masters strenuously warn against having a mirror directly face the main door.

Also be careful when installing mirrors in the bedroom. Most feng shui practitioners are agreed that mirrors should not face a bed, from whatever angle. This is because, seeing one's reflection in a mirror upon waking up might give one a fright, which creates unstable Chi. Another explanation is that mirrors reflecting the marriage bed cause discord and misunderstanding between spouses.

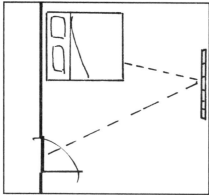

Mirrors can assist in room arrangements. Beds which cannot face the door (for some reason) can use mirrors to reflect the door.

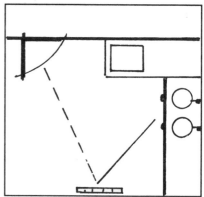

In the kitchen the cook should face the door. If this is not possible, use a mirror to reflect the door. This improves feng shui.

Wall mirrors are superb for reflecting good luck symbols into a home, especially where there is view of water. Here the mirror is placed in the dining area.

MIRRORS

have various uses in Feng Shui. To be used as tools, they should be installed as wall mirrors as shown in the picture here. And they should not be too low as to have the effect of "cutting" off the head of the tallest resident.

Wall mirrors are highly recommended for the dining rooms of homes, as it is believed the "doubling" of food on the table is good symbolism for the home. Wall mirrors are also used to reflect beautiful sceneries from the outside - like a view of a favourable waterway or river into the home.

Mirrors also have multiple uses for those in business, especially when strategically placed to reflect the cash register - again this represents a doubling of revenues for the business. Restaurants are also fond of using mirrors to symbolise a busier environment.

Mirrors are very effective for taking care of columns - wrapping the column with mirrors completely removes the bad effect of its sharp angles. Business premises having this problem are advised to use mirrors. It fans turnover !

Finally mirrors are used to "extend" out walls, so that the effect established is that " missing corner of the house then appears to be recreated.

83. The use of WINDCHIMES to enhance feng shui can be extremely effective when used in conjunction with one or more of the classical formulas associated with the PaKua. Windchimes are made of either bamboo, copper or stainless steel hollow rods hung in groups of eight or five, and with a centre piece that create tinkling sounds each time it catches the breeze. According to feng shui, the creation of this sound encourages Chi to rise through the hollow rods, and then to settle, thereby bringing abundant good luck and prosperity.

Depending on what they are made of, windchimes can represent either the metal or wood element. The beautifully crafted modern windchimes currently available through gift shops are deemed to be of the metal element and are excellent conveyors of good Chi when placed in the West or Northwest sectors, sectors corresponding to the Trigram TUI (small metal) and CHIEN (big metal) respectively.

According to the Eight Life situations of the PaKua, West symbolises the "children's sector" and Northwest symbolises the "helpful people sector." Using a windchime in these corners of your house will enhance these two aspects of your life. Metal windchimes can also be hung in the North (representing the element Water) and this intensifies your career prospects, and opens up new opportunities for you.

Bamboo windchimes belong to the Wood element. These can best be hung in the East (Big wood) and South East (Small wood). These sectors/corners of your apartment or house represent the "Family luck" and "Wealth luck" respectively. Hanging a bamboo windchime in these sectors will seriously activate your luck in these two domains of your life. Also, windchimes are particularly potent for attracting prosperity and wealth. However, a word of warning. Do not hang metal windchimes in your wood element sectors because metal destroys wood !

Bamboo windchimes can also be hung in the South corner of your house. South is of the Fire element, and since wood feeds fire, the windchime will activate the luck of this sector which has to do with one's fame and reputation.

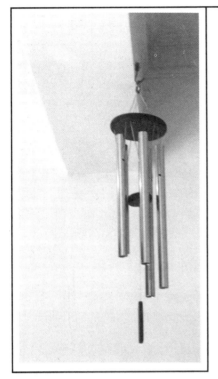

WINDCHIMES

are such excellent tools for enhancing the feng shui of homes mainly because of the tinkling sounds they make each time a light breeze blows - this creates happy vibrant CHI for the household. The hollow tubes (made from copper, brass or bamboo) then channels the CHI upwards thereby ensuring it settles, and brings good luck to the residents.

There has been some misgivings about windchimes. Some people fear that windchimes attract naughty "spirits" into the home, which may harm them. The author wishes to reassure readers that she has had windchimes hanging in her homes for over twenty years with absolutely no problems - indeed many people have been profuse in their thanks for the good luck it has brought to them. In Hong Kong the use of windchimes is very popular with people in business. Just make sure that when you purchase them, that the long cylindrical tubes are hollow, and not solid because this method of feng shui makes use of the channelling technique.

84. The use of LIGHTS is another very effective method of correcting feng shui problems associated with irregular shaped land or rooms. Wherever there is a corner deemed missing, installing a light at the strategic corner happily fills in the missing corner ! Lights also represent the element Fire, and it is the Yang in the Yin Yang representation of feng shui philosophy. It thus has several uses associated with the creation of "balance" and harmony within a household.

Bright lights are particularly important in the entrance areas of the home. These should ideally be kept switched on if the foyer is dark and cramped. Bright lights always attract good Chi flows and many of you would have noticed how you tend to be attracted to restaurants and shops that are well lighted. Such business premises enjoy a brisk trade and usually do very well.

In the house, the best representation of lights is the crystal chandelier. This is because the crystal balls reflect light further enhancing the effect. Such chandeliers should best be placed in the South corner of the home. This is the sector which represents fire and should thus be always kept well lighted. The south also governs the reputation sector, and keeping it well lighted assures residents of maintaining their good name always.

Crystal chandeliers are also excellent when hung in the centre of the home which traditionally symbolises the essence of the household. The centre is of the earth element. Fire produces earth and is thus good for this part of the house.

There are two other earth sectors in any home. These are the South west (big Earth) and North east (small Earth). Hanging chandeliers there will activate the Marriage and Knowledge sectors respectively. Thus if there is a member of the household who wants to get married badly, locate his/her bedroom in the southwest part of the house and then hang a chandelier there.

If you cannot afford a chandelier, hang a very bright light instead, and then try to keep it on most of the time.

Crystal chandeliers like these are excellent for living areas. If you use them in your home make sure they are regularly switched on to create favourable CHI flows for the room.

LIGHTS

These small chandeliers are perfect for lighting up important corners of the house. When using lights to enhance the feng shui of certain corners, select chandeliers with crystal "balls".

85. Colourful, vibrant FLOWERS create happy Chi inside a household. The potency of "good luck" flowers cannot be overstressed and in old Chinese homes, large paintings of peonies, chrysenthemums, magnolias, plum blossoms and other auspicious flowers are a common sight. Flowers are believed to have an uplifting effect on a person's individual Chi, which in turn balances with the Chi of the environment to bring happiness and prosperity, with everything going right.

Although fresh flowers are always preferred, artificial silk or paper flowers are equally effective. At any rate, artificial flowers are better than fresh flowers which have withered and faded ! So for those of you who tend to forget to throw out faded flowers, the solution is to depend on artificial flowers. In this connection it is useful to also mention that artificial trees with fabric leaves are also perfectly acceptable !

But dried flowers are definately a No No ! Make sure the flowers you use are colourful and vibrant, and that they give you a sense of life and activity. Try to select flowers carefully. Orchids and roses and carnations are very sweet, but they do not have the feng shui potency of peonies and chrysanthemums, or of narcissus and plum blossoms. These flowers are believed to attract great good fortune and as such are usually displayed in Chinese households during the Lunar New Year celebrations. You can display them all year round ! The author's home is filled with vases of peonies and plum blossoms (all artificial) which create abundant happiness Chi for the whole family.

Flowers are extremely effective in activating the "family and wealth sectors" of the home - the East and Southeast - both of which directions/locations also correspond to the wood element. Flowers belong to the wood element. They are thus also good for the South - fire - which represents your "good name and reputation sector"

The use of flowers for feng shui purpose can also be extended to offending corners that protrude. Place a large vase of flowers in such corners to deflect the Shar or killing Chi created by the protruding corner.

These artificial peonies are especially effective for enhancing "marriage" corners of the home. Fresh flowers are better, but artificial ones like these are fine. Do not use dried flowers !

FLOWERS

Flowers, natural or made are excellent feng shui enhancers. Placed all over the home, they create happy CHI flows which create harmony and happiness for the household.

These red roses are also artificial. Placed next to crystal ornaments they are very effective for activating a household's marriage luck for eligible sons & daughters.

Flowers also represent the element Wood, and are particularly beneficial for people born in a Fire element year because wood produces fire. Flowers should be discarded when their colours fade, or when they lose their lustre and sheen - this rule applies to both natural or artificial flowers.

To activate the marriage corner, place them in the Southwest sector of the home.

Dried flowers are considered very harmful from a feng shui viewpoint since these symbolise something dying, or dead or dried up from lack of water. Thus elaborate arrangements using dried flowers should not be used for decorative purposes.

86. PLANTS & TREES can be used to cure a whole range of feng shui problems. From blocking off poison arrows, inside and outside the home, to activating specific corners of the home, plants, artificial or live, have a great potency to create, recycle and and cause the accumulation of Chi.

Plants bring balance and harmony to the home because they complement the brick and mortar used to build the house. Plants also represent life and growth, and these symbolise advancement and progress - good feng shui. If you are born under the wood element, or the fire element, plants and trees are especially good for you to have around.

However, Wood destroys Earth and exhausts Water and accordingly plants may not be so auspicious for people born under these two elements. In feng shui terms however, element analysis does not stop at personal horoscopes alone. Equally important is to identify the various elements of the different corners of your home so that you will be able to identify which sectors will benefit the most from having plants placed there.

Obviously the Wood element sectors would be especially good. And these are East and South East, the family and wealth sectors. Putting plants in these sectors will bring in wealth and promote family harmony and happiness.

The author has often been asked to recommend the "best plants" to use for the interiors. For the inside of homes DO avoid the prickly plants like cactus, or plants with pointed thorns. These may be great for the outside - because they can represent protection for the home - but for the indoors, it is not recommended. Instead, go for plants which have round, broad leaves like the money plant and ferns.

There is a story of a man whose restaurant in California was doing extremely well, until he placed two huge pots of cactus at the inside doorway of the restaurant. Within a month his customers had dwindled to the extent that he barely had any business. Business recovered as soon as he removed the offending cactus plants.

Green plants are wonderful for bringing life to corners, and also for deflecting the unlucky Chi created by sharp angled pillars , as shown here.

GREEN PLANTS

One of the best things to introduce into a home are thriving green plants which bring life into tight corners and are also superb for deflecting bad Chi created by columns, beams and other angled corners.

Plants can be artificial, as long as they do not appear sickly or dead. They should also be cleaned regularly, to ensure dust does not build up. Plants that do not grow well or look like they are about to die, should be discarded and replaced by something healthier looking. Also, plants with broad rounded leaves are to be preferred over plants with sharp or pointed leaves.

Green plants are especially good for those born under the influence of the Fire element (wood makes fire), but they also complement Wood element people.

Plants are often used to activate specific corners of the house, depending on what you wish to emphasize. Thus if you want your career enhanced, a good method is to place a vibrant green plant in the North sector of the house, both upstairs and downstairs. Similarly if you wish to activate your wealth corner, place an especially healthy looking plant with broad leaves in the Southeast corner of your house.

This has the effect of creating good quantities of healthy vibrant CHI which attract the kind of luck represented by these corners.

87. The words "feng shui" mean wind and WATER. From time immemorial, water has played a large part in the fortunes of the peoples of China. Water is represented by the life giving rain which cause crops to grow. But water also overflows the banks of China's great rivers bringing floods that cause death and destruction. The Chinese refer to the wrath of dragons when heavy rainfalls cause rivers to break their banks, and they give thanks to benevolent dragons which bring the life giving rain.

So it is with feng shui. Water represents wealth and abundance, prosperity and riches. But only if it is controlled and oriented in the "correct way". Water feng shui is a specialist "branch" of feng shui, and the Water Dragon Classic sets out auspicious and inauspicious waterways, their directions of flow and the effect of their shapes and curves - all in great detail.

For feng shui enhancing purposes, many of the old texts refer to water in the context of the five elements, water being one of these elements. According to the texts, water of course destroys fire and exhausts metal, but it produces wood, and is in turn produced by metal. Using these cyclical flows of productive and destructive relationship, it is then possible to identify the most auspicious locations to place water type structures within a home. These are miniature fountains, artificial waterfalls, aquariums, and fish ponds.

Based on the PaKua's later heaven arrangement, the sectors of the home most likely to benefit from "flowing water" is the North sector. This is represented by the Trigram KAN which is symbolised by water.

The north sector also signifies career prospects for residents, and enhancing this corner of the house encourages favourable luck for one's professional and business pursuits. Using this method of enhancing prospects is especially potent for people born of the water or Wood element, as the harmony extends also to the individual.

Water is also good for the wood sectors ie South East and East, because water produces wood. Placing water in these sectors will enhance family happiness and wealth prospects for the residents.

144

A small to medium sized pond stocked with healthy, active and colourful carp brings harmony and good health to a household. Ponds are good feng shui.

WATER

In Feng Shui water almost always bring good luck, and having a small pond, a fountain, or a fish tank in one's home is always a good idea.

FISH PONDS & WATER FOUNTAINS

Water is good for people born in the year of wood element, because water produce wood in the Cycle of elements. Just one important rule. When building a pond inside the house, make certain it is on the left hand side of your main door (ie taking your direction looking out). Otherwise your husband will have more than one wife, or at best, have a tendency to have a roving eye.

Locating the pond on the left is also auspicious from a wealth perspective. Such ponds are believed to attract money luck.
Do not, however be tempted to make your pond too large, since too much water can create imbalance and instead of attracting good luck, the excess water could end up "drowning" you.
Remember, in Feng Shui, balance is vital.

145

88. Feng shui enhancement also extends to the outside of homes, but this aspect of the practice refers more to protection than enhancement. So far we have made much of the importance of main doors and entrances to one's home or office. This main door needs to be "protected" at all times. According to feng shui practice there are several ways this can be done.

The traditional approach to creating some kind of protective aura for the home is to place a pair of stone lions outside the gate. But there are other methods and other "tools" which can be used.

The most famous and well known of the protective tools is the eightside PaKua symbol. This can be purchased from most shops selling joss sticks and other prayer paraphernalia. The PaKua symbol that is used for protection is made of wood and painted in red, with the eight Trigrams drawn around the symbol.

For feng shui purpose, please look for the PaKua which has the Trigrams arranged in the Later Heaven sequence. This is used for Yang dwellings ie homes of the living. The PaKua which has the Trigrams arranged in the Early Heaven Sequence is meant for use on gravesites of ancestors, called Yin dwellings. The PaKua symbol should have a small round mirror in the centre for it to be potent as a symbol of protection. Hang the PaKua above the main door in the centre. The author generally does not encourage the use of the PaKua symbol as there appears to be a certain amount of supernatural phenomena attached to it thereby requiring it to be chanted upon and "blessed" by a monk. Sometimes the Pakua may not be strong enough and may thus fall off. It is therefore advisable to use some other tool for "protection".

The author has found other protective symbols very effective, objects like brass cannons, fierce animals done in ceramic or wood or portrayed in paintings, and even sharp triangular objects pointed outwards, although anything which "hurt" others should be avoided. It can tempt retaliation, and negative Chi created can recoil backwards. Also useful are prickly plants placed as a pair just outside the main gate of the home. These guard against malevolent spirits.

SYMBOLS OF PROTECTION

While the Feng Shui of homes and offices are continually being enhanced, it is also important to devote some attention to creating symbolic protection for the household.

The Chinese like using fierce animals to protect their homes, and the famous stone lions often seen at temple gates is vastly popular and can be easily purchased from any Chinese Imports shop.

This is a painting of the legendary white eagle of Northern China - believed to be fiercely protective. It is an excellent painting to use as "protection" for the home.

In addition to the stone lions, another popular animal used is the tiger which is believed to be so fierce that it is sometimes dangerous to use his picture when there are members of the household born in the years of small animals (rabbit, chicken, sheep, even pig) which represent "food" to the tiger.

In view of this, Feng Shui masters recommend the use of paintings of fierce protective birds, and one such bird is the eagle, shown here with an intimidating expression. Hung just outside the main door, it serves to protect the house against petty burglars, and also protect residents from people whose intentions may not be honourable. Such people cannot stay too long in the house as they will feel uncomfortable.

When using paintings such as these to symbolise protection, you should refrain from hanging them inside the house as they are supposed to "guard" the house againsts outsiders. Putting them inside the home can turn them against residents.

PART THREE
SPECIAL FENG SHUI APPLICATIONS

Chapter 7
FENG SHUI for CAREER SUCCESS

89. Take a systematic and focused approach when attempting to use feng shui to enhance personal career prospects. After reading all the literature you can lay your hands on about feng shui, it is possible you could end up quite confused, especially when confronted with contrary advice.

Over the years the author has personally "tried out" every new formula or method which has come her way. The approach taken is mildly scientific, rather than based on blind faith. After making the calculated or recommended changes, she follows this up with a period of careful observation - to detect the flow of luck, and the subtle changes hoped for, or promised. This enables her to "test out" the potency of the recommended changes, so that over time it is possible to observe what works and what does not, and more important, which method seems more powerful given the context of a particular situation.
The reader practitioner is strongly advised to take a similiar approach. If career success is what you want, these are the rooms/structures you should check out immediately:

* Focus on your BEDROOM.
  Check the direction and positioning of your room; your bed and your sleeping position. Apply the various methods and formulas contained in this book to make these observations.

  Check the element of your bedroom sector, and how you can best enhance the feng shui of your bedroom sector, using element analysis. Use the productive/destructive cycle.

  Next, check the exact spots in your bedroom which correspond to the career success corner based on the PaKua Trigrams. Then activate this corner with suitable feng shui enhancing tools.

* Focus on your DRESSING TABLE or AREA
  Check the direction you are facing when you get ready for work each morning, making sure you observe the subtle Chi flows caused by corners, layouts and other furniture.
* Investigate the feng shui implications of your mirror.

* Focus on your OFFICE at work
Check your office table, its position, direction and dimensions.
Initially, concentrate on the general guidelines of good feng shui, and
then only, go deeper by working out your best directions and
locations based on the PaKua LoShu formula, a summary of which
is given in Chapter Nine.

If you want more details of this formula you are recommended to
study this particular method of feng shui elaborated in the author's
book on the subject. This is a particularly potent formula which has
brought a great deal of success to those who have practised it. It is
potent because it identifies the four good and the four bad directions
based on your personal birth chart.

In the same book there is also a chapter on auspicious dimensions
and these are especially useful when measuring the size of your
desk. The author kept getting promoted at her job after she had
ordered a new desk, made to specific feng shui dimensions !

Also undertake thorough element analysis of your room or corner
vis a vis the whole office. This enables you to decide on how best
you can enhance your particular office or corner, and more, how you
can also zero in on the career corner and activate it.

It is also possible to use the same PaKua evaluation of your office
in the same way as you do for your bedroom at home. This helps
you identify your favourable and crucially important corners

* Focus on your DOORS
  Check the main door to your house.
  Check the door into your bedroom.
  Check the main door into your office.
  Check the door into your office room (if any).

There are specific feng shui rules governing the most auspicious
location, direction, size, positioning, and orientation of doors. Once
you have familiarised yourself with these rules, check out your
doors thoroughly, and if there are problems, introduce feng shui
"cures" recommended to regularise the flow of Chi..

90. Focusing on the BEDROOM requires analysis of your bed location. But first make sure the shape of your bedroom is regular. If it is not, make the necessary adjustments recommended in earlier chapters. Next, make certain your bed is positioned with you diagonally facing the door. If you sleep with your back to the door you will be symbolically encouraging people to work against you behind your back ! Do not sleep with your head directly pointed at the door either, because if you do all your advancement luck will "stagnate and die". And certainly do not sleep facing the attached toilet/bathroom. This puts you directly in the path of ill fated Chi coming from the toilet. You will have loads of problems at the office !

Three of the taboos of "sleeping feng shui" which have a direct bearing on your career prospects are summarised in the diagrams here. These supplement your information on bedroom feng shui dealt with earlier. In addition, if you sleep under a beam or with a protruding corner pointed at you, you can expect to be blamed for mistakes, you can expect quarrelsome colleagues and hostile bosses and you can expect quite a bit of severe headaches !

After you have swept your bedroom clean of all the feng shui bugs, you can start to introduce some enhancing features into the room. Make sure your bedroom is well lighted if you read or work there. Place a bright light in the career corner of your room ie the north sector. If you can, also place a metal windchime in this corner since anything metal in this corner will help activate your career prospects.

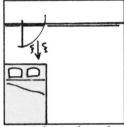
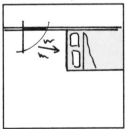
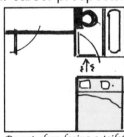

Do not sleep with your head directly pointed at the door.	*Do not sleep with your back to the door. Bad !*	*Do not sleep facing a toilet or bathroom. Bad !*

91. You should also investigate which sector of the house or apartment your bedroom is located in, and, using the fomula given in Chapter Nine determine whether you are located in at least one of your four good directions. Based on this formula, you will have great success if your are in your best sector, but if you are not, and you cannot move to another more auspicious room, try moving your bed to that part of your room which represents a good corner for you, and even more important make sure you can sleep with your head pointed towards your good directions. This enables the good luck chi to flow into your head even as you sleep, thereby attracting success for you.

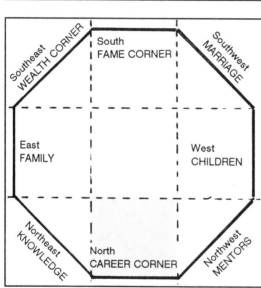

Locating your "favourable corners" inside your bedroom requires you to superimpose a PaKua symbol onto the room and then identifying the directions/sectors.

Having identified your favourable corner in your bedroom, it is a good idea to place your bed or table in this part of the room, making sure at the same time that you are also sleeping and facing the auspicious direction. All this may appear really troublesome and inconvenient, but the efforts are often worthwhile, and they are inconvenient only during the initial period. Once the bed and the table are set up, observe over a period of about three months and if you see that your luck at the office has improved, in that working life becomes more pleasant and you are getting noticed more, then you know that you are indeed tapping into your good directions very effectively. If however, the results are discouraging, eg if after the change you sense increased hostility at the office or you see opportunities passing you by, check your directions once more.

92. The orientation of the DRESSING TABLE in the BEDROOM affects career progress because this is where early morning Chi affects a person. If you are facing your best direction when you put on your face each morning, the energy flows created will be positive, and will have a positive impact on your career.

Your auspicious directions are easily determined by referring to the PaKua LoShu formula in chapter nine. Try to place your dressing table in a way which enables you to tap your best directions. But Do also consider some of the "taboos' of feng shui ie that ideally the mirror should not be facing the bed, or be at the foot of a bed.

It is preferable that the dressing table, with its accompanying mirror be in a separate annexe of the bedrrom, or if this is not possible, even be in the toilet.

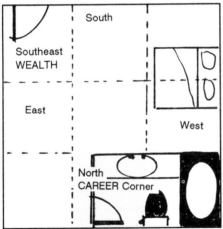

The location of this toilet in the north sector of this room is extremely unlucky for the resident's career. Far better if he changes to another room.

While on the subject of toilets DO make very certain that the toilet you use is not in the North sector of the house; nor should it be in the North corner of your bedroom. This has a direct unlucky and inauspicious effect on your career, since toilets located in the north are interpreted as "flushing away all your career prospects".

Also refrain from placing a plant in the North sector since a plant here represents wood which exhausts the water of the north.

Likewise, anything representing earth (like natural crystals, boulders etc) will be detrimental to the career corner. This is because earth is believed to destroy water. Under the element relationship formula therefore, wood and earth are incompatible with the career corner. But metal or gold is good for it, and indeed will enhance the career corner. Thus copper or brass windchimes would be quite ideal.

93. Examining the feng shui of the OFFICE involves much detailed investigation (ask colleagues about the background of rooms assigned to you) and requires the use of a compass to determine directions. At the work place, directions and locations take on meaningful significance for one's career prospects. If your office is inauspiciously located, you will definately suffer from backbiting and poor prospects, and even perhaps get the sack. Certain desks and chairs in some offices even come to be referred to as "jinxed" chairs in that whoever occupies it invariably ends up getting sacked. On the other hand there are also "lucky rooms" which bring luck to all who occupy these rooms in that they all go on to better things and higher positions.

The author used to have an extremely favourable room location while working with the Hong Leong group in Malaysia. Not only was it located in the furthest diagonal corner to the entrance door (a favourable orientation), it also had excellent unencumbered views of the city. In addition the direction of her room door was facing her best direction, and her desk was easily moved around to again face her best direction. When she capped it all by ordering a new desk, made to exact feng shui specifications (in terms of height, length and breadth and number of drawers), her career started to really take off. In that year she enjoyed multiple promotions and a significant rise in income and recognition.

After her transfer to Hong Kong, colleagues who "inherited" her office and her desk also benefited tremendously from the good feng shui created by her feng shui master.

To improve the feng shui of your office, first make sure you are not sitting underneath exposed beams and that you are not being hit by sharp corners. next make sure you are not sitting with your back to your door (you will be stabbed in the back !); You should also not have your back to a window, otherwise you are lacking in support. If there is a view of a benevolent hill place it behind you as it will give you wonderful solid support and protection.
If you like you can also hang a small windchime either at the entrance to your office or at the northern corner of your office.

If you have inherited a "good" office, in that the former occupant has moved on to a promotion or to better things, leave things as they are for about three months. Sometimes an office enjoys good feng shui because of its naturally good feng shui situation. At other times however an office may be good for one person but not so good for someone else. Thus a certain amount of patient investigation and observation is needed.

Good or bad feng shui manifests itself in the way your work is received/regarded by your bosses, in the way you inter relate with colleagues and co workers, and in your health and energy levels. If you continually get sick, or if quarrels seem to flare up for no obvious reason, or if your boss appears continiously hostile, then you could have reason to suspect that perhaps something is wrong with the feng shui of your office.

There is also a time dimension to feng shui.

According to the ancient texts on the subject, the feng shui of dwellings and places cannot continue to enjoy good feng shui forever; that indeed, the luck of a place actually does change every twenty years. There are thus 20 year cycles to take account of.

To determine whether a place has good feng shui from a time perspective require very detailed calculations that are based on the MOVING STARS method of feng shui. As this is a very complicated branch of LoShu feng shui requiring intensive study, this aspect of feng shui has not been included in this book, although the author plans to deal with the subject in her next book - one which explains feng shui using numerology formulas of the LoShu grid or magic square, and marrying these numbers to the number of the present twenty year period which runs from 1984 to 2003.

The novice practitioner need not yet concern himself with the time dimension. If you feel that your office room is somehow "not quite right" and is not giving you good feng shui, try activating it according to your auspicious directions, based on the PaKua LoShu formula.

After a while you will definately see some results.

94. To investigate the feng shui quality of your desk location and your seating arrangement, it is useful to superimpose the PaKua onto your office room, and from there use a compass to identify the career and wealth corners, ie the north and the southeast respectively. These are the two corners of the room which have a direct bearing on your career feng shui. These locations, are supposedly the "corners" which should be activated if you wish to enhance your career potential.

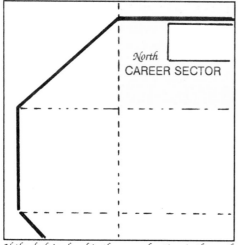

If the desk is placed in the career location, ie the north sector of the room as shown here, and this corner gets activated, eg with a windchime (metal producing water), it is auspicious.

In the example shown on the left, the North sector of the office has been identified. This is the career corner. Placing a desk here is good and if the corner is also activated by placing an object which represents metal (eg a copper or stainless steel windchime, old Chinese coins, or something made of gold) in this corner, perhaps on the desk or hung above it, then the room becomes auspicious for advancing careers.

Alternatively if the door to the room is located in this sector it is also regarded as auspicious for career advancement. The important thing to note is that the sector must get "activated" for the full potential of the sector to be manifested in the form of good luck Chi flows. This is done by identifying the element which symbolises the sector and then enhancing it accordingly.

In the example above, following the PaKua's Later Heaven Arrangement, North is represented by the element Water and thus metal is good for the sector. Alternatively, any of the water enhancing tools (aquariums, miniature fountain) will be equally effective.

95. The direction you face when you work in the office has a very major effect on your career luck. If you sit facing an auspicious direction, you will be clear-headed, calm and resolute when working, thinking, and making decisions. These attributes, together with the merging of your personal Chi with that of the environment will bring you good luck. To check your auspicious and most favourable directions please refer to Chapter nine for an explanation of the PaKua LoShu feng shui method.

Much of the dilemma facing practitioners is to decide how they can best "tap" their auspicious direction(s) without also at the same time spoiling other feng shui features.

Usually when confronted with a predicament of this nature, feng shui Masters recommend going for the second and third best directions - the contention being that no matter how "lucky" a direction is from a personal horoscope viewpoint, if other aspects of landscape feng shui are ignored, the results will be unsatisfactory.

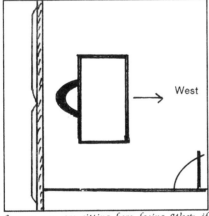 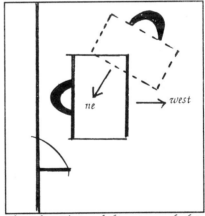

Suppose you are sitting here facing West; if West should be your best direction, you will benefit greatly provided your back is not to a window. If it is try tapping your second best direction.

If you face West, and this puts your back to the door, even if West is your best direction, the position is not auspicious. Try tapping other "west" directions ie SW; NW and NE.

96. Having checked the location and the direction of your desk, the next thing to do is to check your desk DIMENSIONS. Yes there are good and bad dimensions and certain dimensions are more auspicious than others, especially for people who wish to create good feng shui for their work - be it for careers, for management advancement or for business. The auspicious dimensions have to be carefully calculated based on the feng shui ruler which spells out in detail the exact type of good and bad luck for various dimensions. The author's book on Applied PaKua LoShu feng shui has a chapter dealing with the feng shui ruler. For working desks however readers may want to consider the dimensions suggested here.

LARGE DIRECTORS DESKS
An excellent measurement for a very large desk suitable for company directors and chief executives would measure 33 inches high; 60 inches long and 34 inches wide. If the table is too high for you, place a small platform underneath your chair to raise the level of the chair. This dimension given is excellent for senior managers who have to work harmoniously with his/her staff. It is very conducive to attracting career luck.

MEDIUM SIZED MANAGER'S or EXECUTIVE'S DESKS
A smaller size desk which is auspicious would be 33 inches high, 48 inches long and 32 inches wide. Again if you are too short for such a desk, use a raised platform for your chair. This height is very auspicious and is highly recommended.

THE SECRETARY'S TABLE
should not be L shaped please !! Instead it should be a regular rectangular shaped table. The perfect dimensions for secretaries desks will be 33 inches high, 68 inches long and 26 inches wide.

Try not to have book cases with open shelves around you. The shelves represent unfriendly "blades" hitting at you. If you need to have a book case, the recommended dimensions are 68 inches high, 43 inches wide and 18 inches deep.

97. The next step in your pursuit of auspicious career feng shui is to check all the important DOORS which you use regularly, as these doors affect your personal fortune. These include the main door to your house/apartment and office building; the door to to your bedroom and study or work room at home, and the door to your private office room. All the rules and guidelines regarding doors apply when you assess your entrances, and some of the more important things to look out for are summarised here.

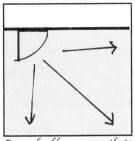

Doors should open correctly to the large area of a room.

Doors with see through glass panes are bad.

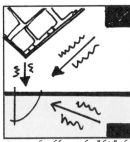

Doors should not be "hit" by poison arrows of any kind.

First make certain that nothing "killing" is pointed or directed at any of your doors. There should also not be blockages which hinder the smooth flow of Chi into your various private rooms. If you do discover "hidden arrows" take steps to diffuse, deflect or divert the shar Chi coming from these arrows. Block them off with plants. Deflect bad Chi with circular or moving things like windchimes. And as a last resort use the powerful PaKua mirror symbol or miniature cannons.

Next compare the size of your door(s) with surrounding doors and make certain they are all aligned in a balanced manner. Make sure your door(s) are not facing a staircase, a lift, an elevator or a toilet. And ensure that your door is neither too large nor too small.

Doors should open correctly, ie into the room rather than against a wall. Change the hinges if there are doors like this. Main entrances should have proper doors, not glass sliding doors that look more like secondary doors. This reduces their potency.

98. The LOCATION and DIRECTION of ENTRANCES also have the potential of creating auspicious (or inauspicious) luck to benefit your career. This can be investigated by analysing the various corners of your office and home. Since you wish to activate and enhance your career prospects, having your main entrance door located in the North sector of the office/home would be auspicious. In an office building, if you find that there is more than one entrance to the building select the one that is more auspicious for you (by checking the PaKua LoShu formula in chapter nine) and then use this entrance daily. The same reasoning also applies if there is more than one entrance to your main office and your home. By using an auspicious door, your luck will tend to improve.

The author knows several important and successful businessmen in Kuala Lumpur who head large corporations that have impressive head office buildings, but rather than enter or leave by the main entrance way, they use the side entrances. This is because they have been advised by their feng shui consultants that the orientation of the main entrance way is not auspicious for them (even it may be auspicious for their companies !). It is useful to remember that companies also have birth dates which differ from that of the big boss ! At the same time, since there is also a time dimension to feng shui, an entrance which may have been auspicious when the building was first built, say ten fifteen years ago, may no longer be enjoying the same good luck orientation today !

Managers and executives who enter their building through the car parks in the basement should check out the direction of the entrance to the car park, since this then becomes their main point of entry and exit from the building each day. For public entrances the orientation of the entrances will have different effects on different people. However their location and direction will determine the overall luck of the building and its occupants. Thus buildings which have their main doors un-encumbered, and located in, and facing the South east would generally be tapping the wealth sector of the building. This is interpreted by feng shui experts as being generally auspicious as long as other features are also favourable.

Chapter 8
FENG SHUI for BUSINESS SUCCESS

99. There are many different ways to enhance feng shui for business success - from methods aimed at increasing turnover at retail establishments and restaurants, to formulas directed at increasing prosperity luck for businessmen and offices. Feng shui features, introduced in factories also improve employee productivity and work flows. The business people of Hong Kong and Taiwan regularly introduce feng shui features to their business establishments, and many would not make major structural of interior design changes without consulting the feng shui man. Perhaps that is why commercial enterprises tend to be so successful in these countries ?

The Chinese businessman of the old school does tend to be superstitious. Many faithfully observe customs and practices which have been handed down from previous generations - respecting the good luck rituals of the lunar new year for example, keeping old premises deemed to be lucky, hanging on to certain numbers which have been identified as propitious, and perhaps most of all, following the doctrines of good dates and bad dates as laid out in the "Tong Shu" - the Chinese Almanac that is based on Chinese astrological calculations of suitable and unsuitable days, while at the same time orienting their homes and offices according to auspicious directions and locations.

These practices, rituals and customs are all inter related. And to the businessman, feng shui is regarded as perhaps the single most important factor NOT TO IGNORE when they set up new establishments or move to new premises either for residence or for expanded commercial activities.

In Hong Kong, taxi driver and tycoon alike hold similiar reverence and respect for feng shui. The same holds true for the Chinese of Taiwan, and increasingly in recent years, of Singapore and Malaysia as well. There also seems to be a major revival in interest in this ancient science, to the extent that even western educated new generation scions who manage inherited businesses today subscribe to an acknowledged potency in feng shui.

The author has personally heard highly educated, much exposed and widely travelled corporate personalities repeatedly concede that good feng shui had ostensibly opened up profitable opportunities for their companies, and that feng shui had contributed to the smooth implementation and success of specific operations within their corporations.

They acknowledge that tapping into the wisdom of this ancient science can be pleasantly rewarding. The great enticement is that often, very little up front cost is required. The harnessing of auspicious feng shui requires relatively insignificant investment in monetary terms. Nor does it require any major compromise of values or religious beliefs. Feng shui can be treated as a science. Nothing more.

To a commercially minded person therefore, having invested funds to start up a new business, it makes sense to also make the effort to "tap into the Chi flows of the earth", if that is what it takes to harness a little bit of luck as well ! Just as feng shui can enhance one's personal happiness, increasing the prosperity potential of one's life, so can it be harnessed to aid one's commercial businesses.

As with residential dwellings, the process starts with "cleaning and protecting" business places from the effects of killing Chi caused by all sorts of pointed and hostile structures. Protect the front doors. Block off hidden poison arrows. Where necessary retaliate with a strategically positioned PaKua mirror or a cannon.

From there it is then possible to proceed to activate the wealth sectors of business places - ie the South east corners of offices, factories and retail establishments. If possible have the cash register, or accounts office where billings and collections are done, to be located in the South east. In other words every aspect of your business which deals with cash or profitability should be located in this wealth sector.

If you like, it is also possible to enhance the wealth sector by installing water in the sector - an aquarium with live fish to symbolise growth or a small revolving fountain to represent continious turnover - because water of course creates wood, the ruling element of the Southeast.

100. If you wish to expand the size of your TURNOVER feng shui Masters advice making use of old CHINESE COINS. These coins represent gold (the ancient representation of wealth and income), and their symbolism can be "tapped" to the advantage of your business. The method involves tying three old coins together with auspicious red thread and then sticking the coins on top of your invoice books and order books.

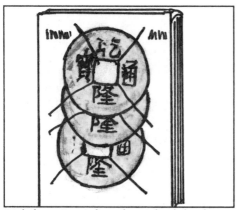

Stick three coins, tied together with red thread on top of your invoice or order books to increase turnover.

There are several variations of this recommendation. You can also use eight coins to "double" the effect of the coins, or you can hang replicas of these coins on the wall of the sales manager's office, or you can display them on your desk.

Proprietors of retail establishments can also create pathways of stepping stones designed in the shape of coins leading up to the main entrance of their shops in a symbolic gesture to attract "wealth to the front door".

Hang eight coins tied with red thread in the sales manager's (or branch manager's) office.

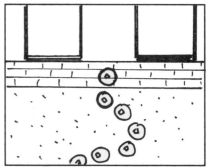

Create a pathway of "coins" leading to the entrance of your shop to increase business.

SOME INFORMATION ABOUT COINS

Coins have always been a symbol of prosperity in ancient China, and the usage of old and antique coins as amulets and for feng shui purposes is fairly widespread even up until modern times. Ancient Chinese Coins are round, and with a square hole in the centre. Tied with auspicious red thread the Coin is regarded as a very potent symbol for attracting excellent business and wealth luck. The symbol of the coin, shown in the sketch here is also one of the most popular of the so called Eight Treasures !

Old Chinese coins symbolise prosperity and wealth and are popular feng shui symbols for enhancing business.

In addition, antique coins are also highly prized. Carried on the person or worn and sewn onto tunics they are supposed to bring good luck to the wearer.

Coins of the TANG and SUNG Dynasties are also in great demand as amulets and ornaments, or worn as protection against poverty. Imitations, sold by street vendors are available in the night markets of Hong Kong. Genuine coins can be found in Kuala Lumpur's central market.

Coins are believed to be powerful talismans for attracting auspicious business luck. Hanging ten antique coins tied together with red thread over shop doors is supposed to attract wealth to the establishment. Another use of coins is to design the driveway towards one's main door in a formation of old coins ie several round patterns with a square in the centre. A trail of coins to one's house symbolise the flow of wealth to one's front door. It is believed that a single coin hung on a red thread will acquire potency when first placed near the God of Wealth for a short period of time, and subsequently worn around the neck or displayed. This supposedly attracts business opportunities. Some parents also string coins together for their children to wear to ensure a stable & prosperous future for them.

This practice is based on word of mouth superstition and is part of the tradition of magic connotations practised under the broad influence of Taoism.

101. Another widely acknowledged method of enhancing business turnover, especially of retail establishments is to focus some feng shui techniques on the CASH REGISTER. Locate it in an auspicious corner of the shop. Make sure it does not face the main door directly, or a toilet, or the kitchen. Ideally it should be near the entrance doorway, but not directly facing it. Have it backed against a wall for solid protection and install a mirror on the side wall, thereby reflecting it. This represents a doubling of turnover. It is also auspicious if the cash register is placed in the Southeast corner of the shop as this is the wealth sector.

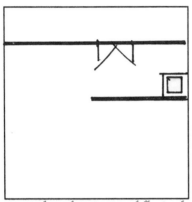

Locate the cash register carefully. In the foyer area but diagonally opposite the entranceway, is an auspicious location.

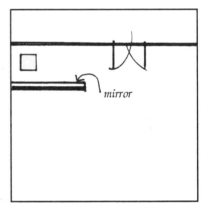

Having a mirror reflect the cash register is a favourite ploy used by restaurant owners of Hong Kong to increase customers.

It is possible to further enhance the feng shui of the cash register by placing the three coins tied with a red thread on the sales book placed nearby. An alternative method is to hang two flutes above the cash register in a way which has the flutes slanting towards each other thereby simulating the PaKua shape.

These flute should be tied with red thread and have the mouth part at the bottom. This method uses the channelling method to create prosperity Chi for the cash register. The flutes encourage chi to flow upwards, and to settle around the area of the cash register thereby causing it to "fill with money".
The methods on this page are popular with Hong Kong retailers.

102. If yours is a RESTAURANT BUSINESS, it belongs to the fire element, because of connotations related to cooking. For such businesses the feng shui of the kitchen is vital and the important thing to remember is that the cook(s) must not have their back to the door while cooking. This creates unbalanced Chi which is bad for business. Restaurants that have a great deal of red in their decor tend to do well because it complements the natural element of the business.

Another excellent feature for restaurants is the use of lights. Well lighted restaurants have the power to "pull in the customers" and to gain a solid reputation. Check this out by driving around the city. You will see that most of the brightly lighted restaurants (some to the extent of being gross and gaudy) do a booming business. Again this is because lights belong to the same element of fire. Dimly lit restaurants seldom do as well; but do differentiate between a restaurant and a bar/pub which belongs to the water element - in such cases red, and bright lights is most unsuitable. The complementary colour is black or dark blue. Hence it is preferable that such establishments be dimly lighted.

Restaurants which have wall mirrors to symbolise a busy doubling of customers also do well. As do restaurants which display live fish (for eating!) swimming in a glass case, but these should be carefully placed in either the north (water); east or southeast (both wood, and water produces wood) sector of the restaurant.

The direction of the entrance to restaurants should be auspicious for either the owner or the cook; Or it should correspond to the fire element - south. This ensures success for the restaurant.

Finally, it is auspicious for restaurants to display large figurines that depict happiness and a full tummy. It is for this reason that Chinese restaurants often display a large (sometimes lifesize) statue of the laughing Buddha, complete with his fat prosperous tummy.

The Chinese believe that the laughing Buddha has the power to attract a lot of customers into the restaurant.

103. If your business has to do with **REAL ESTATE** - buying and selling of houses and apartments; or if you are engaged in the development of real estate; or if you are an architectural firm or a contractor, then the element representing your business is earth. You should therefore try to activate the earth sectors of your office. This corresponds to the centre of the office or to the southwest and northeast sectors. Locate the people crucial to your business in these corners and also proceed to activate the earth element in these sectors. This is done with the use of feng shui enhancing tools. Activate earth with natural quartze crystals, or stone/marble carvings displayed in the relevant corners.

104. If your business has to deal with cash and money, - **BANKS, INSURANCE & FINANCE** companies, money changers, your business element is water, which corresponds to black and blue. Such companies do well when they incorporate these colours into their decor or logo. In addition their business premises should be softly lighted, and should also make use of the water enhancing tools for feng shui. The best location for such businesses is the south sector of their halls & offices, which represents water. Also, because metal produces water, windchimes are excellent enhancement for such businesses.
Other businesses represented by water include trading, shipping and travel.

105. If yours is a JEWELLERY business, your element is gold, or metal and the use of windchimes would be ideal for your business. Activate the west and northwest corners of your establishment. Do not use red in your decor because fire destoys metal. But do use the three coins method to "churn up business" - for some reason it is supposed to be especially useful for jewellery shops.
Other examples of metal type businesses are mining companies, engineering firms, car assemblers and sales offices, machinery and equipment enterprises, and so forth.

106. Businesses which fall into the wood element category are PLANTATION, FARMING, PAPER and other businesses which involve plants - both live and artificial. FURNITURE companies and SAWMILLS etc are also part of the wood element. The wood directions are east and southeast. These are the favourable sectors for such businesses.

In delineating the "favourable sectors" based on the PaKua's Early Heaven Arrangement of Trigrams (as we have done here), it is essential to take the analysis a step further. The favourable sectors are based on the element(s) representing the trigrams. In addition, practitioners are also urged to study the productive or destructive relationships of the elements and use the feng shui enhancing tools accordingly.

It is necessary to stress that while PaKua feng shui decrees certain corners and sectors of a room to be "favourable", the feng shui quality of surroundings must also be taken into account. Thus, even if the main door of your business is facing a favourable direction and located in a lucky sector, it may still not be good feng shui if the door itself is being hit by shar Chi.

Businesses which are affected by shar Chi suffer lost opportunities, have problems with authorities, and suffer a range of other difficulties, sometimes severe enough to seriously affect the survival of the business.

The practitioner should also note that feng shui is a dynamic science which does not stay static, and that business feng shui is affected, not by any single force but rather by several merging forces, which must be kept in balance and harmony. Thus earlier references to Yin Yang balance, and the element harmony should be considered together rather than separately. This concept of balance and element complementarity can be extended to other aspects of a company's "face" ie its signboards, its logo and even the calling cards of its managers. Good feng shui requires an integrated approach, and the feng shui of offices of key personnel should also be analysed and treated to benefit the company.

107. The layout of desks in TRADING ROOMS for those engaged in the various dealing businesses - STOCKBROKING, COMMODITY & CURRENCY TRADING - is believed to exert strong feng shui repercussions. The author knows of banks and stockbroking companies which have benefited from re arranging the furniture in their dealing rooms after consulting the feng shui man. The general principles to follow are simple - ie avoid pointed angles hitting at the chief dealer(s); get away from L shaped and U shaped arrangements of desks; do not have the desks with their backs to windows or the doorway and other easy to follow guidelines dealt with in earlier sections of the book.

It is also advisable to pay some attention to desk dimensions of dealers tables. In any financial institution, the dealing boys' direct contribution to the bottom line of the firm can be either astronomically profitable or dangerously loss making. Mistakes are very costly, and even where firms have stringent systems of control and rules against the taking of open positions, substantial losses can still be incurred.

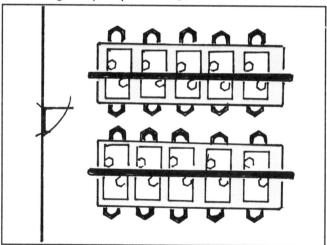

For dealing rooms, the regular layout shown above is preferred to elaborate U shaped or T shaped arrangements.

Modern day dealing rooms are a hub of activity, with c o m p u t e r terminals and consoles on every desk. make certain none of the dealers are being "hit" by o v e r h e a d b e a m s o r stand alone s q u a r e columns.

108. Be very alert to dangerously sharp corners or structures on the shop floor, in the main halls or in the various "important" offices. These should be covered or disguised with fake plants and creepers. Besides, trees create a feeling of springtime and symbolise a time of growth and expansion. Use the various feng shui enhancing tools freely and see your business grow !

Smalltime businessmen and shopkeepers of Chinese origin in Asia are very fond of displaying "good luck symbols" on their business premises. They believe that these symbols attract good business luck and bring wealth and prosperity. The most popular symbols are pictures or statues of their respective Gods of wealth, and abundance. In Hong Kong, many division heads and supervisors freely display good luck dieties, and even a highly professional, westernised corporation like the Hong Kong Bank has witnessed its officers hanging pictures of the God of wealth in their offices !

Merchandisers and Window dressers of department stores can also benefit from a few feng shui "tips". The author once used a bunch of fake trees (with silk leaves but genuine branches) to launch the start of the spring collections at her department store in Hong Kong. The trees were strategically placed "to grow out of sales counters and cashiers desks" on all the floors of the main store. Turnover during that month doubled !

Yet again, when she organised the grand launching of her megastore Home & Design centre, she strategically placed "dragon crystals" all over the shop floor and had bright down lights aimed on these dragons ! The lights created rainbows all round when it "hit" the faceted crystals, thereby creating massive quantities of sheng Chi. The Home Centre was profitable from day one - a rare feat in the world of retailing ! Customers kept being "pulled in" by a strategically placed windchime hung at the entrance to the store, while impressive wall mirrors were installed at all the cash registers throughout the store.
The Home & Design Centre had been an important experiment in feng shui to help the business (at very little extra cost). It worked, and it created a favourable impact on the bottom line.

109. Shop entrances should be carefully designed to "attract" customers, and doors should not be too small as to impede entry, nor too large as to allow Chi to flow right out again. Display cabinets inside the shop should not have the sharp ends pointed at the entrance way. This has the effect of hitting customers thereby discouraging them from entering the store.

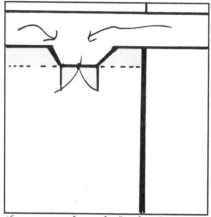

Shop entrances designed to "welcome" customers are auspicious. Here the doorway resemble open arms and is auspicious to attracting customers.

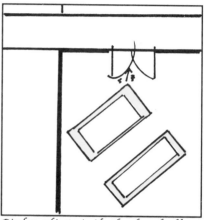

Display cabinets inside the shop should not have sharp edges pointed at the door. This discourages customers from entering.

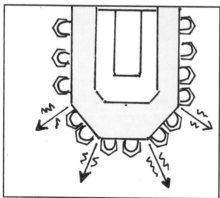

Pubs should not have bar tables that have sharp edges. They should be rounded. Angles cause discord & financial difficulties for owners.

In fact all retail businesses can benefit from "symbolic" decor. It is advisable to select auspicious colours(based on element analysis) and also to display good luck symbols. All the images that convey "wealth, longevity and peace"; as well as the characters that denote "double happiness, long life and prosperity" are suitable for business premises. Work them into the decor of your shop, showroom or office. Be as creative as you wish !

PART FOUR
SPECIAL TECHNIQUES & FORMULAS

Chapter 9
* EAST HOUSE WEST HOUSE
  THEORY of FENG SHUI
* EIGHT LOCATIONS
  THEORY OF FENG SHUI
* PA-KUA LO-SHU
  FORMULA of FENG SHUI
* EIGHT LIFE SITUATIONS
  THEORY of FENG SHUI

THE MANY THEORIES & METHODS of FENG SHUI

The fascination and challenge of feng shui lies in its many theories, methods and interpretations.

There is landscape school feng shui which base the science on the contours of the physical landscape - mountains and rivers - their shapes, sizes and courses. Auspicious and inauspicious sites are compared to highly symbolic representations of the four celestial animals - the dragon, the tiger, the turtle and the phoenix - while areas of abundance and prosperity are likened to sites that are replete with the Dragon's cosmic breath - the vital Chi. landscape feng shui depend on one's powers of observation, and an analysis of one's guided imagination.

And there is compass school feng shui which adopts a more mathematical approach. Theories and methods of the latter school are more complex, and are generally based on the eight sided PaKua symbol with its Later Heaven Arrangement of the I Ching's Trigrams. This evolved into the geomancer's compass.

These theories were also founded on the nine sector LoShu magic square with its arrangement of the numbers 1 to 9 in the nine squares in a way generally believed to possess powerful influences over the fortunes of the Universe.

There are many versions of these feng shui theories. Some are static requiring exact measurements of directions while others are "moving" ie adding a time dimension to good and bad luck.

This chapter highlights summaries of some of the more popular theories used by the feng shui masters of today.

EAST HOUSE WEST HOUSE THEORY OF FENG SHUI

This theory of feng shui maintains that the eight directions of the eight sided PAKUA symbol contains eight HOUSES. These can be divided into two categories of four houses each ie the EAST houses and the WEST houses. The names of the houses, their front and back directions and their elements are summarised here for easy reference. Please study the tables carefully.

THE FOUR EAST HOUSES
HOUSE NAME

Li	Back: South	Front: North	Element: Fire
Kan	Back: North	Front: South	Element: Water
Chen	Back: East	Front: West	Element: Wood
Sun	Back: S.East	Front: N.West	Element: Wood

THE FOUR WEST HOUSES
HOUSE NAME

Chien	Back: N.West	Front: S.East	Element: Metal
Kun	Back: S.West	Front: N.East	Element: Earth
Ken	Back: N.East	Front: S.West	Element: Earth
Tui	Back: West	Front: East	Element: Metal

To identify the kind of house you have, first check the direction of your front and back doors. Take these directions from the inside looking out. When in doubt use the BACK door to be the determining factor as to what type of house it is.

Example: If your back door faces N.West while your front door faces S.East, yours is a *Chien* House. It belongs to the West Group of houses and its element is Metal.

Example: If your back door faces South and your front door faces North, yours is a Li house. It belongs to the East Group of houses and its element is Fire. If the front door faces North and the back door faces S.West it is a Kun House (and not a Li house) belonging to the West group of houses. Under this method of feng shui it is the back door that determines what house it is.

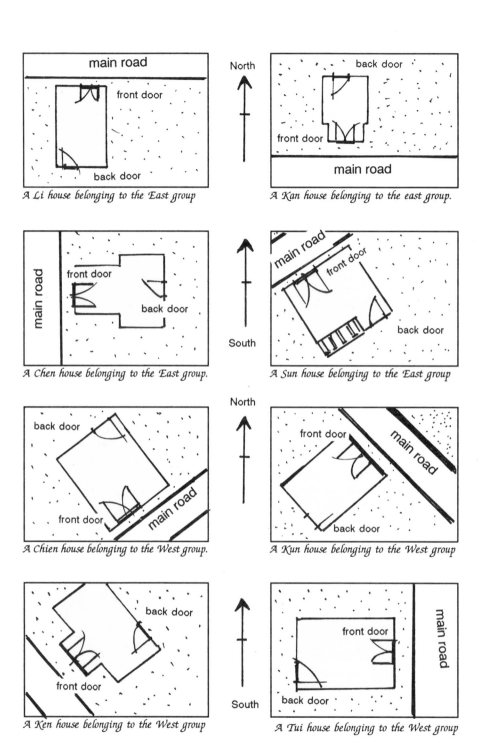

A Li house belonging to the East group

A Kan house belonging to the east group.

A Chen house belonging to the East group.

A Sun house belonging to the East group

A Chien house belonging to the West group.

A Kun house belonging to the West group

A Ken house belonging to the West group

A Tui house belonging to the West group

176

EAST GROUP HOUSES belong to the elements water, wood and fire. These houses are in a harmonious relationship with each other since water produces wood which produces fire. East group houses clash with West group houses because the elements are in a conflicting relationship eg the metal of a West house destroys the wood of the east house.

The feng shui of East group houses can be enhanced with plants, flowers, bright lights and water structures like fountains, fish ponds and aquariums. Place these enhancers near the front door, or in the corresponding element sectors.

WEST GROUP HOUSES belong to the elements metal and earth. The houses are in a harmonious relationship with each other, but clash with the East group houses. To enhance the feng shui of West group houses, use windchimes and crystals.

There is a further dimension to the analyses.

Like houses, people too are divided into East and West group people. It is possible to investigate whether your house is good for you by investigating whether you are a West or an East group person.

To find out whether you an East or West group person, this method offers a summarised table which is reproduced on the next page.

Check your year of birth against the indicated Trigram, and from the Trigram indicated you will not only know whether you are an East or a West person, but also exactly which direction(s) your front and back doors should be facing. East group people should live in East group houses and West group people should live in West group houses.

Thus if you are a West group person living in an East group house, it cannot be very auspicious, and vice versa. The best arrangement is to have a perfect match, thus if you are KAN person, live in a KAN house and if you are a CHIEN person, make sure you live in a CHIEN house ie that your house is facing Southeast in front, and is sitting with its back to the Northwest.

From the table below, match your relevant YEAR of birth to the TRIGRAM to determine what kind of house is best suited to you.

CHIEN:(West group)
Male: 1940,49,58,67,76,85
Female: 1946,55,64,73,82.
KUN: (West group)
Male: 1941,44,50,53,59,62,68,71,77,80,86,89.
Female: 1942,51,60,69,78,87
KEN: (West group)
Male: 1947,56,65,74,83
Female: 1945,48,54,57,63,66,72,75,81,84
TUI: (West group)
Male: 1948,57,66,75,84
Female: 1947,56,65,74,83

LI: (East group)
Male: 1946,55,64,73,82
Female: 1940,49,58,67,76,85
KAN: (East group)
Male: 1945,54,63,72,81
Female: 1941,50,59,68,77,86
CHEN: (East group)
Male: 1943,52,61,70,79,88
Female: 1943,52,61,70,79,88
SUN: (East group)
Male: 1942,51,60,69,78,87
Female: 1944,53,62,71,80,89.

If your door orientations do not suit you, try to re-orientate their direction to improve your feng shui. If your front door faces a direction belonging to a West house and your back door faces a direction which belongs to an East house, you can decide which type of house is better for you and then make the changes accordingly. Obviously an East group person should strive to live in an East group house and vice versa. If the Trigram cannot match exactly, try to get the east or west group to match.

EIGHT LOCATIONS THEORY OF FENG SHUI

This method of feng shui focuses on the interiors of houses. According to this theory, every house can be divided into Eight locations, with each one of the locations corresponding to one of the eight sides (or directions) of the PaKua.

Each of the eight locations have certain characteristics which may be auspicious of inauspicious, and the good and bad loactions differ according to what kind of house it is. here when we refer to 'kind of house" we are referring to whether it is a west house or an east house, and more specifically which of the trigram rules the house. We have found out from the west house east house theory that this depends on the location of the back door. Before analysing the quality of the eight locations of your house, you must first determine what kind of house yours is.
It is then possible to identify the "good" and "bad" locations of each of the eight types of houses.

THE GOOD LOCATIONS

THE MAJOR LOCATION: It coincides with the back door of the house and is suitable for bedrooms and altars. The stove should be placed in a direction that is directly opposite the best location.

THE HEALTH LOCATION: Excellent. This part of the house brings good health and energy. Good for dining rooms and for bedrooms of family members who may be ill.

LONGEVITY LOCATION: Good for older members of the family.

PROSPERITY LOCATION: Excellent. This is the prime location for creating wealth opportunities and for bringing prosperity to the household. This is the most auspicious location for the front door, master bedroom, the study or any area associated with your work or business, and it should be kept well lighted, clean and vibrant.
Do not place your toilet or kitchen in this location.

THE BAD LOCATIONS

THE DIFFICULTIES LOCATION: signifies the area of the house which cause legal entanglements, disputes, quarrels, anger and irritations. Do not locate any of the important rooms (eg bedrooms, study etc) here. It is suitable for toilets and store rooms.

THE LOSS & SCANDAL LOCATION: signifies an area which generate laziness, listlessness and loss of energy. It is suitable for the toilet, the store rooms or the kitchen.

THE OBSTACLES LOCATION: symbolises loss, theft, burglary, being cheated, being betrayed, legal entanglements and financial loss. Suitable only for toilets and kitchens.

THE DEATH LOCATION: signifies accidents, poor health, fatal illnesses and disease, misfortunes of a grave nature, loss and death.

According to this method of feng shui, internal layout of rooms and interior decoration can benefit from a knowledge of the characteristics of each location.

Once you have identified these areas in your house, do not fret or worry unduly if you find that you have a toilet, say in the prosperity location. Or your bedroom located in the difficulties location. These things can be modified. Effects of locations can be reduced or enhanced.

Thus if you do have a toilet located in the prosperity area try to reduce using that particular toilet. Keep the toilet door close, or better still, depending on which element is represented by the location, display a symbol there which represents or "produces" this element.

If your bedroom is located in the difficulties location, change your bedroom, and if this is not possible, then make certain you are at least sleeping in a way which allows your head to be pointed in the prosperity direction eg if your prosperity location is Northwest, and your bedroom is located in the Northeast, it belongs to the same West group of directions. So it is compatible. Sleep with your head pointed to the Northwest to draw on the prosperity of that direction.

Here are the "good" and "bad" locations of the eight houses.

A CHIEN HOUSE
(Back door: Northwest)
MAJOR location is N.West.
HEALTH location is N.East.
LONGEVITY location is S.West.
PROSPERITY location is West.
DIFFICULTIES location is S.East.
LOSS & SCANDAL location is North.
OBSTACLES location is East.
DEATH location is South.

A KUN HOUSE
(Back door: Southwest)
MAJOR location is S.West.
HEALTH location is West.
LONGEVITY location is N.West.
PROSPERITY location is N.East.
DIFFICULTIES location is East.
LOSS & SCANDAL location is South.
OBSTACLES location is S.East.
DEATH location is North.

A KEN HOUSE
(Back door: Northeast)
MAJOR location is N.East.
HEALTH location is N.West
LONGEVITY location is West
PROSPERITY location is S.West.
DIFFICULTIES location is South.
LOSS & SCANDAL location is East.
OBSTACLES location is North.
DEATH location is S.East.

Here are the "good" and "bad" locations of the eight houses.

A TUI HOUSE
(Back door: West)
MAJOR location is West.
HEALTH location is S.West
LONGEVITY location is N.East.
PROSPERITY location is N.West.
DIFFICULTIES location is North.
LOSS & SCANDAL location is S.East.
OBSTACLES location is South.
DEATH location is East.

A LI HOUSE
(Back door: South)
MAJOR location is South.
HEALTH location is S.East.
LONGEVITY location is North.
PROSPERITY location is East.
DIFFICULTIES location is N.East.
LOSS & SCANDAL location is S.West.
OBSTACLES location is West.
DEATH location is N.West.

A KAN HOUSE
(Back door: North)
MAJOR location is North.
HEALTH location is East.
LONGEVITY location is South.
PROSPERITY location is S.East.
DIFFICULTIES location is West.
LOSS & SCANDAL location is N.West.
OBSTACLES location is N.East.
DEATH location is S.West.

Here are the "good" and "bad" locations of the eight houses.

A CHEN HOUSE
(Back door: East)

MAJOR location is East.
HEALTH location is North.
LONGEVITY location is S.East.
PROSPERITY location is South.
DIFFICULTIES location is S.West.
LOSS & SCANDAL location is N.East.
OBSTACLES location is N.West.
DEATH location is West.

A SUN HOUSE
(Back door: S.East)

MAJOR location is S.East
HEALTH location is South.
LONGEVITY location is East.
PROSPERITY location is North.
DIFFICULTIES location is N.West.
LOSS & SCANDAL location is West.
OBSTACLES location is S.West.
DEATH location is N.East.

From the details above the reader can observe that "good" and "bad" locations follow their east and west characteristics. Thus the East directions - South, North, East and Southeast are all good for you IF you are an East group person; and the same goes for the Eest group directions - Northwest, Southwest, West and Northeast - being all good for West group people.

Once you have mastered the theory behind this particular method, you will find it very easy to make the element co-relations, and based on feng shui enhancing tips and tools presented in earlier chapters you will eventually be able to enhance each of your good locations, and also reduce the bad effects of your bad locations.

PRACTICAL TIPS FOR IDENTIFYING HOUSES

It should be obvious by now that the key to identifying houses, and from there, determining the characteristics of the various locations depends on correctly recognising back doors and front doors. In olden days this was a relatively easy process. In modern day house designs however, it can sometimes be tricky trying to pinpoint exactly which one is the front or back door, especially since some buildings have as many as four doors, and some houses have several secondary doors that may be patio doors and sliding doors. Exactly identifying the back door therefore can be difficult. Here are some interesting guidelines offered by practising feng shui masters.

* Based on the scenerios of olden days when properly sited houses were backed by mountains and faced rivers, modern day practitioners can substitute big buildings for mountains and roads for rivers - so that the direction of the house or building facing the main road is then regarded as the front of the house and the opposite side considered its back. So if in doubt, look for where the main road is. Even if there IS a main door on the side of the house facing a side street, that cannot be regarded as the front of the house !

* It is also believed that the true front of the house is where most of the favourable Chi can concentrate and gather. This is the side of the building which faces either a main road or a broad expanse of unbuilt land like a park, an open space, a children's playground, or a pedestrian mall. Where there is such an empty space facing one side of your house or building this is considered the front of the house, and the back is then the opposite side. Even if there is a "main" door at a side street of the house or building, that cannot be regarded as the front of the house.

* In rare instances of irregular or unusual shaped houses or buildings eg L shaped or Y shaped houses, the house is regarded as having no common front and back doors. The way round this problem is to consider each wing or arm of the building as independent entities which have then to be examined separately. Such houses at any rate are not recommended since they suffer from a lack of focus. Without there being a clearly defined entrance front door causes favourable Chi to be easily dispersed and lost to the house.

PRACTICAL TIPS ON DEFINING THE EIGHT LOCATIONS

When defining and attempting to measure the eight locations of a house or building, the first thing to do is to draw a floor plan of the house. This must be drawn to scale as measurements of demarcation must be very exact. Next find the centre of the house, draw a square around the center and divide it into eight equal sectors. Match each of the sectors according to the compass reading which identifies both the DIRECTION and the LOCATION.

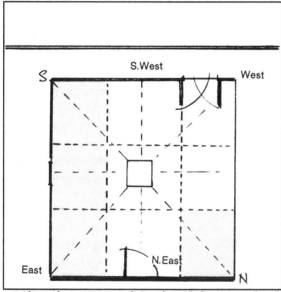

Dividing a house into its eight "good" & "bad" sectors is done by identifying the compass directions. This is a KEN house because its back faces Northeast.

Please note that while the example given here refers to a house, the same analyses can be done for a building, an entire shopping complex, a whole country or a small room !

There are no space limitations and restrictions in the application of feng shui theories because the influences of feng shui are directional. They apply equally to small areas and to large areas.

Once you have succeeded in identifying the "good" and "bad" locations, it is a simple enough matter to arrange the layout of your rooms and work areas to ensure that you get maximum benefits from feng shui forces. If you are unsure which member of your family should benefit most from the arrangement of rooms, check the birth years of all members of the family to determine the respective compatibility of each member's ruling Trigram with each of the rooms. Notwithstanding all of this however, do bear in mind that according to Chinese tenets, the feng shui of a house should first benefit head of the household, from whom all good things emanate.

One major difficulty of application arises when the building or house being investigated is not symmetrical in shape and where the so called "centre" may lie outside the building itself. Or when there is no clear centre. Examples of the latter situation arise in buildings which are L shaped, U shaped or X shaped. The best way to get round the problem of analysis in such instances is to demarcate the buildings into two or more separate parts before attempting to centralise and identify the eight locations. This is shown in the diagrams below.

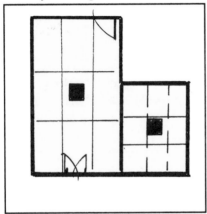

This L shaped house is divided into two separate parts of eight sectors each.

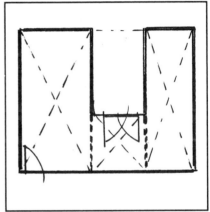

This U shaped building is divided into three parts of eight sectors each.

Do try and match your personal Trigram or Kua to that of your house. Having said this however, it is acknowledged it is not always easy or possible to change an east house into a west house and vice versa.

What do you do then, if you are an East group person and you have to live in a West group house ? Does this mean your feng shui will definately be bad ? The answer is Yes, the house is generally not auspicious for you. However, this does not mean you cannot do anything about it. Improve your feng shui by rearranging room layouts to suit you and IGNORE the type of house it is. Identify your personal Kua based on the Table on Page 177 and then identify your four "good" and "bad" locations. Then proceed to use the good locations for your important rooms and work areas.

Example: If you are a CHEN person (East group), your excellent locations are South, East, North and S.East. Even if you live in a West house, your feng shui luck improves if you sleep in the South sector.

Finally, it is necessary to address the practical difficulties associated with actual layout of floor plans and rooms. Obviously it is impossible to utilise only the good locations in a house. One cannot place all the beds and all the doors of the house only in the four good locations.

In the same manner it is not possible to have only toilets and store rooms in the bad locations. The entire exercise becomes even more complicated and impossible if there are equal members of the household belonging to both East and West groups ! What is good for one group becomes, by the definations of this particular theory, bad for the other.

Thus in a family of four, two members may belong to the East group and two members belong to the West group. How does such a family organise the house then ?

The solution is to COMPROMISE !

Compromise is possible if you can define exactly what is most desired by the family. Is it wealth ? Is it health ? Is it the achievements of the Children ? Is it family harmony, a good marriage ?
Then tap the relevant loction(s) which deal with these accordingly, for each member of the family. To each according to his wants !

Next, determine who is the most important member of the family. Often this person is the family patriarch, who is also the main breadwinner. Sometimes however, it may be the mother, or the eldest brother, or the eldest son. Whoever this person is, his feng shui should be given important consideration !

Not all rooms or doors have equal importance in feng shui. It is possible to rank these structures and furniture according to the influence they exert on one's luck. Thus for feng shui purpose three things are vital to get right ! These are the location (and direction) of the Main Doors(front & back), the Bedrooms, and the Cooking Stove.

If there is a conflict of interest between husband and wife because both belong to different groups, then the main doors and the stove should be oriented to benefit the husband while the bedroom should be oriented to benefit the wife.

THE PA-KUA LO-SHU THEORY of FENG SHUI

This theory or formula, believed to be extremely potent if accurately followed, is presented in depth in the author's book " Applied Pa-Kua Lo-Shu Feng Shui". The theory is briefly summarised here, but readers who are keen on going deeper into the formula and its multiple applications are invited to get a copy of the book.

Pa-Kua Lo-Shu Feng Shui, as the name suggests, is based on the two premier symbols of Chinese Feng Shui practice - the eight sided Pa-Kua and the nine sector Lo-Shu magic square. According to detailed formulas, it is possible for every individual to identify his or her four auspicious and four inauspicious directions. The theory is very similiar to the two previous theories presented in this chapter.

According to the Pa-Kua Lo-Shu theory, every abode can be divided into nine sectors, eight corresponding to the eight directions of the compass and the eight sides of the Pa-Kua, and one in the centre. Each of the sectors represent one of eight auspicious or inauspicious situations and these are categorised as follows:

THE AUSPICIOUS LOCATIONS

SHENG CHI: means "generating breath". It is the best location for attracting wealth luck, for getting your timing right, for money luck, and for attracting great prosperity. If you are a politician activating or tapping your Sheng Chi location will attract a high and honourable position for yourself. If you are a student it will bring examination and scholarship luck and if you are a businessman it will bring wealth luck. To tap the Sheng Chi, locate your bedroom, study and/or your front door in the location representing it.

TIEN YI: means "doctor from heaven". It is the best location for members of the household who may be sick or suffering from severe health problems. Tien Yi is exceptionally potent in curing prolonged and inexplicable illnesses. The best method of tappin the Tien Yi location is through the siting of the family stove. Position the stove with its source of energy (the fire-mouth) facing the Tien Yi direction.

NIEN YEN: means "longevity with rich descendents". It is the location for enhancing the quality of home life and family relationships - between husbands and wives, parents and children and between the siblings. The Nien Yen location should be tapped if the family is suffering from too much internal squabbles and bickering; or are unable to have children. It is also favourable if grown up children are having a hard time finding suitable marriage partners. And finally it is an excellent location to site the master bedroom if husbands and wives are growing apart ! Indeed the Nien Yen is excellent as a cure-all for all manner of family problems and difficulties.

FU WEI: is the location for overall harmony and peace. It is favourable for the maintenance of good fortune and for leading a comfortable life, although with nothing spectacular in terms of abundant wealth or business success. Fu Wei offers better than average luck - a most favourable livelihood, more boys than girls in the family (in the old days sons were considered a manifestation of good luck !) and strong protection against unfavourable luck. But nothing more than this.

THE INAUSPICIOUS LOCATIONS

HO HAI: means "accidents & mishaps". This location leads to disasters, some loss of money, and intermittent difficulties and frustrations. However it is the least unlucky of the four inauspicious locations. A store room here would be quite right !

WU KWEI: means " five ghosts". This location generates the kind of bad luck which results in fire, burglary, loss of income, and loss of employment. It also causes quarrels and misunderstandings between family members and between you and your friends and colleagues. Wu Kwei cause mischief at home and at work. You can suppress the five ghosts by having your toilets sited in this location.

LUI SHA: means " six killings", and as this implies it is a location that represents grievous harm to you and your family; it also symbolises missed opportunities at work and for your business. Lui Sha cause legal entanglements, illnesses, accidents and even, in a worst case scenerio, death. Again, toilets in this sector suppress the evil vibes of the sector. You can also render the sector totally ineffective by having your store room located here.

CHUEH MING: means "total loss of descendants", which to the Chinese mind represents the worst possible disaster or bad luck which can befall a family. This is the worst of the eight locations, and feng shui practitioners should make every effort not to locate the main door (or master bedroom) in this sector. If bad luck comes as a result, it is the most severe form of bad luck - like loss of children, loss of wealth, bankruptcy, and/or very severe and chronic illness. Chueh Ming brings tragedy and disaster, it is deadly and fatal. Every effort must be made to suppress it with a toilet/bathroom located here. It can also be suppressed by having the kitchen here, although the direction of the stove or oven should face a favourable direction.

SHORT CUT METHOD OF LOCATING YOUR KUA NUMBER
Master Yap Cheng Hai has given the author a short cut method of locating your KUA number for the purposes of determining your auspicious and inauspicious locations as listed above.

The formula is different for males and females, and for the calculation to work out right, you MUST adjust your year of birth if you happen to be one of those born just before the lunar new year. For example if you were born in January 1946, but your birth was before the lunar New Year of 1946, then you should use 1945 as your year of birth for the purposes of this short cut formula. For those who are uncertain counter-check through your animal sign which changes only after the lunar New year.

FOR MALES:
1. Take your YEAR of birth
2. Add the last two digits
3. Reduce to a single number
4. Deduct from 10. The answer is your KUA number.

EXAMPLE: Year of birth = 1936.
        3+6=9 and 10-9=1
        So the Kua number is 1

EXAMPLE: Year of birth = 1948
        4+8=12; 1+2=3;
            10-3=7
        So the KUA number is 7

FOR FEMALES:
1. Take your YEAR of birth.
2. Add the last two digits.
3. Reduce to a single number.
4. Add 5. The answer is your Kua number.

EXAMPLE: Year of birth = 1945
          4+5=9; 9+5=14; 1+4=5
          So the KUA number is 5

EXAMPLE: Year of birth = 1977
          7+7=14; 1+4=5;
          5+5=10=1
          So the KUA number is 1

After you have calculated your KUA number, you will be able to identify your four auspicious and four inauspicious locations. Each KUA number identifies these locations specifically, and these can be summarised for easy reference in the pakuas below, where the favourable locations are shaded and named according to their meanings, and the unfavourable locations are unshaded.
Please note:
For MALES the KUA number 5 corresponds to the number 2.
For FEMALES the KUA number 5 corresponds to the number 8.

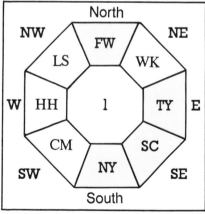

KUA number 1.

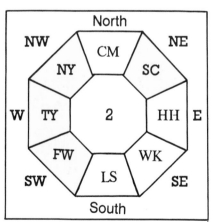

KUA number 2

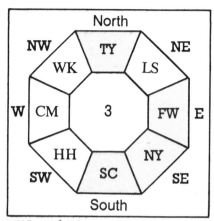

KUA number 3

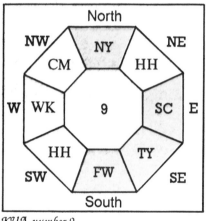

KUA number 9

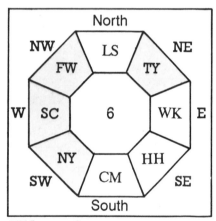

KUA numer 6

Readers should differentiate between LOCATIONS and DIRECTIONS. Thus rooms should be located in an auspicious location and must face the an auspicious direction. However, the direction is taken from inside the room/house looking out. This sometimes give rise to mistakes. So do be careful when implementing any changes to your doors or houses.

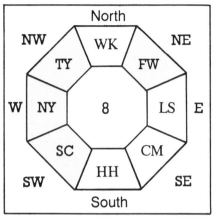

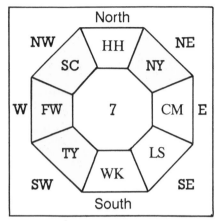

KUA number 8   *KUA number 7*

Readers please note that the eight diagrams orientate the direction North on top. This has been done for ease of reference only. Chinese compasses orientate the South as being on top. When checking the various locations it will help if directions are carefully noted

The actual locations are coded as follows:

THE AUSPICIOUS LOCATIONS (shaded)
Sheng Chi = SC; Tien Yi = TY; Nien Yen = NY;   Fu Wei = FW;

THE INAUSPICIOUS LOCATIONS
Ho Hai = HH;   Wu Kwei = WK; Lui Sha = LS; Chueh MIng = CM;

According to Feng Shui practitioners, once you have successfully identified the good and bad feng shui characteristics of the various sectors and corners of your house, you are then in a position to design your layout and room allocations in a way most beneficial to you, and to other members of your family.

Application of the theories must be practical, and readers are strongly advised not to go overboard by reconstructing rooms and front doors. Usually, if you think things through there are always simple solutions to non alignments of Kua numbers & mismatch of east and west groups.

THE EIGHT LIFE SITUATIONS OF THE PA-KUA

The source philosophy and symbolism of much of the science of Feng Shui takes its cue from the ancient I Ching. Thus the principal symbol of Feng Shui practice is the 8 sided Pa Kua, around which many old formulas have been formulated, many of which can be seen to be variations of each other. Initially, those approaching the subject for the first time can get easily confused, or are rendered uncertain which theory to follow in cases of doubt. The best approach is to be as scientific as possible ie try one method and see whether it works, or better still try to see all the methods as components of the whole practice and take a total approach by trying to marry the theories together. This can be done if one's understanding of the elements, and the basic principles of harmony and balance are always borne in mind.

It is also important to recognise that almost all of Feng Shui is symbolism. Thus the 8 sided PaKua's eight sides each represent many different symbols, from colours to directions to objects and elements. Most significant of all are the TRIGRAMS represented by each side because it is from the TRIGRAMS that much of the meanings take on significance. These TRIGRAMS themselves portray many different characteristics, and for those wishing to delve deeper into the science of Feng Shui, these TRIGRAMS, and by extension, the I Ching must be studied in some depth.

Therefore, how these TRIGRAMS are placed around the Pa-Kua becomes extremely crucial.

It is generally accepted that for the design of good feng shui for YANG DWELLINGS ie dwellings of the living (as opposed to dwellings for the dead - graveyards and tombs), it is the PA KUA arranged according to the Later Heaven Sequence which must be followed. This is because it is this arrangement which pertains to the living abodes of the earth.

The Early Heaven Sequence arrangement of Trigrams refer to heavenly forces which exert their influence on the dwellings of the dead. They do not apply to earth living feng shui.

Thus all the PaKuas illustrated in the author's series of Feng Shui books use the Later Heaven Arrangement of Trigrams.

From this Arrangement has come a very useful and potent method of enhancing various life situations. Thus each of the eight sides, and by extension each of the compass directions, is said to represent one important life situation, and it is further said that the eight life situations thus represented form the sum total of the aspirations of mankind.

By activating or enhancing the particular corner or direction represented by each of these eight sides one is able to focus specifically on a particular area of one's life which represent the things that one wants ie wealth, health, fame, recognition and so forth.

Practising Feng Shui Masters, especially those in Hong Kong are very familiar with this formula which is reproduced here:

CHIEN or N.West governs the presence of helpful people or mentors.
KUN or S.West governs marriage prospects and marital happiness.

CHEN or East governs family relationships and health.
SUN or S.East governs wealth prospects and prosperity potential.

KAN or North governs prospects for advancement in careers.
LI or South governs fame potential, and one's high reputation.

KEN or N.East governs attainment of knowledge/educational honours.
TUI or West governs the luck of children, the next generation.

To find out which corner of your home or building or business premise represents the life situation you wish to activate, use a compass to determine the orientations of your house, and from there proceed to activate the relevant corners by using the various methods dealt with in earlier chapters.

When doing this exercise, study the Pa Kua illustrated on the next page carefully, since this gives you the clues necessary to activate specific corners. Analyse the elements of each sector, the directions and the how these interact with the plants, the colours and the furniture of your house or office. Go for harmony !

THE PAKUA
Arranged in the Later Heaven Sequence

Use the various symbols represented on each side of the PaKua to analyse the feng shui of the different corners of your home or rooms. each of the symbols belonging to each Kua or side are said to be in harmony with each other, and are therefore complimentary. Use the element relationships to determine productive and destructive cycles. And finally, use the PaKua to understand the various theories presented. To practise feng shui for your home, superimpose the PaKua onto your house plan and begin your analysis !

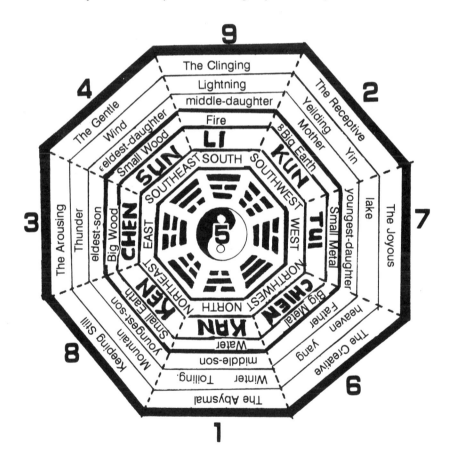

196

THE FENG SHUI SERIES
by
LILLIAN TOO

The introductory book on Feng Shui.
Readers are invited to enter into
the world of dragons and tigers
and to share the secrets of the
Chinese business tycoons of Asia.

Why do some families prosper more than others.
Why does one restaurant flourish,
And another does not …
Why do some companies enjoy robust growth,
While others diminish and weaken …
Why does affluence occur so easily for some people
While ruin and bankruptcy befall others …

The Chinese believe Feng Shui offer potent explanations.
They believe that positive and negative fortunes arise from
auspicious and inauspicious Feng Shui.
Today, interest in this centuries old Chinese wisdom
and practice is going through a spectacular revival.

In Hong Kong, Singapore and Taipeh, three of the world's most
commercially successful cities, Feng Shui is a principal consideration
when businessmen build their homes or construct their offices.

They believe that getting their Feng Shui right will create
abundance and prosperity for themselves and their descendants.

With such promise,
can anyone afford not to know about Feng Shui ??

THE FENG SHUI SERIES
by
LILLIAN TOO

The second book on Feng Shui.

Which reveals the secrets of the powerful
PA-KUA LO-SHU formula,
a potent branch of the Compass School.
The formula pinpoints each person's
four auspicious and
four inauspicious directions.

AND

explains how these can be
applied to one's homes and offices.

The highlight of this second book
is to share
a very powerful Compass School formula
that uses Compass directions

to align individual chi flows
with that of one's surroundings

and in the process
tap into the luck of the Earth
and achieve abundant prosperity
and great wealth …

THE FENG SHUI SERIES
by
LILLIAN TOO

The fourth book on Feng Shui.

Introduces the
Time Dimension
to the Practice of Feng Shui

AND

explains the intangible forces
of the
Flying Star
School of Feng Shui

CHINESE NUMEROLOGY
IN
FENG SHUI

explains the significance
of changing forces
during different time periods.
The formula highlights the influence of
NUMBERS
thereby adding vital nuances
to the practice of Feng Shui

THE FENG SHUI SERIES
by
LILLIAN TOO

The fifth book on Feng Shui

An advanced manual on
WATER FENG SHUI
based on the Water Dragon Classic.
This book reveals the secrets
of the Classic and contains
the old formulas for determining
the correct flow of water.

When precisely oriented and built in accordance with
FENG SHUI calculations, the correct flow of water
brings great abundance of money and wealth luck.